Kiddiwalks

IN
SHROPSHIRE

Judy Smith

COUNTRYSIDE BOOKS
NEWBURY BERKSHIRE

COUNTRYSIDE BOOKS
3 Catherine Road
Newbury, Berkshire

To view our complete range of books,
please visit us at
www.countrysidebooks.co.uk

ISBN 978 1 84674 187 6

Designed by Peter Davies, Nautilus Design
Produced through MRM Associates Ltd., Reading
Typeset by CJWT Solutions, St Helens
Printed in Thailand

Contents

Area Map Showing the Locations of the Walks

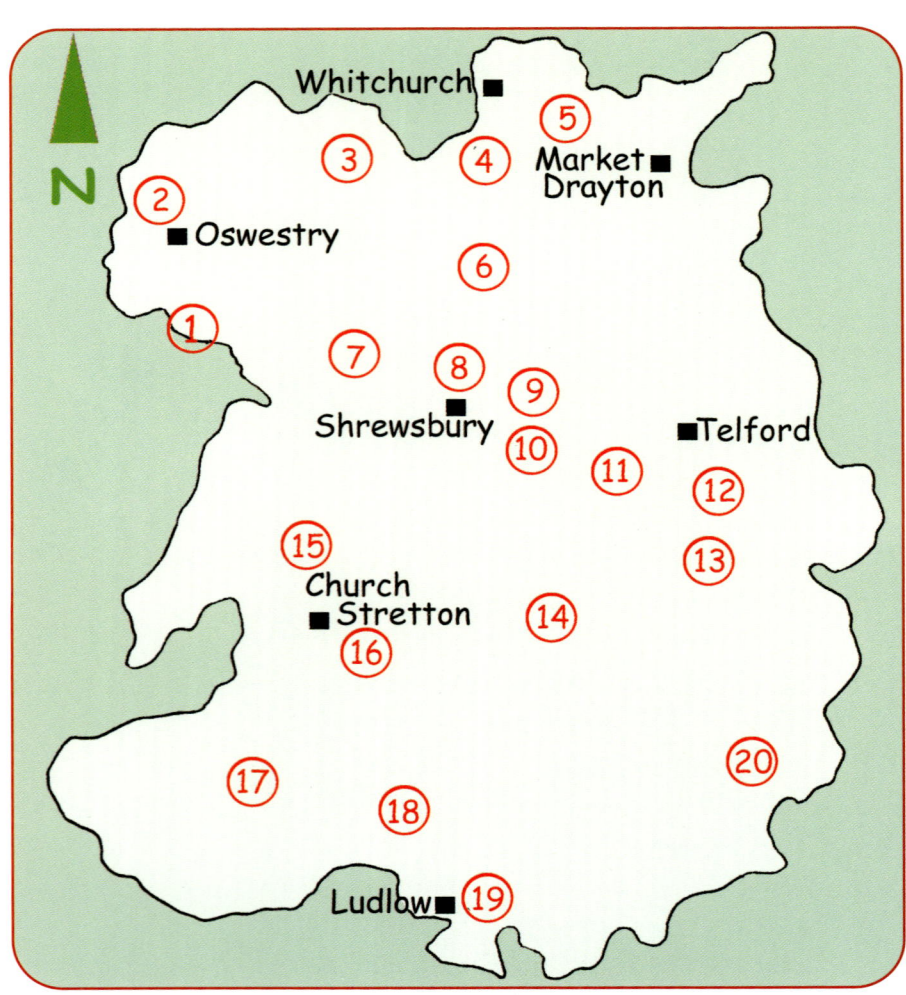

Contents

PUBLISHER'S NOTE

We hope that you obtain considerable enjoyment from this book; great care has been taken in its preparation. Although at the time of publication all routes followed public rights of way or permitted paths, diversion orders can be made and permissions withdrawn.

We cannot, of course, be held responsible for such diversion orders and any inaccuracies in the text which result from these or any other changes to the routes, nor any damage which might result from walkers trespassing on private property. We are anxious though that all details covering the walks are kept up to date and would therefore welcome information from readers which would be relevant to future editions.

The simple sketch maps that accompany the walks in this book are based on notes made by the author whilst checking out the routes on the ground. They are designed to show you how to reach the start, to point out the main features of the overall circuit and they contain a progression of numbers that relate to the paragraphs of the text.

However, for the benefit of a proper map, we do recommend that you purchase the relevant Ordnance Survey sheet covering your walk. The Ordnance Survey maps are widely available, especially through booksellers and local newsagents.

Introduction

Shropshire is a wonderful county for walking. The meres and canals in the north, the sandy banks of the Severn in the east, the tiny villages of the Clun valley in the south, and the wild ridges of the Long Mynd and Stiperstones in the centre are all crying out to be explored on foot. But what sort of outdoor rambling can possibly appeal to a young family? The answer, of course, is that short routes packed with as much juvenile interest as possible are needed – after which it's a good idea to have a few extra tricks up your sleeve as well. Games to play on the way and things to look out for or to collect will all make a walk more stimulating. This book aims to supply some ideas!

It isn't easy for young children to understand why you would 'go for a walk' because that is exactly what they are doing all day anyway! It can encourage little ones if the walk has a special purpose, like going to see the friendly ducks and geese at Ellesmere or to spot the huge dragonflies on Whixall Moss; to find a real highwayman's cave on Nesscliffe Hill, or to track down the beautiful deer at Attingham. Some of the walks in this book have the added interest of little coloured arrows or footprints the children will enjoy following, while others perhaps have lots of appealing wildlife, or maybe a particular story or legend attached to them. Of course it is all the better if there are also rocks to climb, banks to run down, streams to paddle in, and just possibly an ice-cream shop to complete the day!

For children growing up a little, there are also walks here that offer an element of challenge. Everyone enjoys the achievement of reaching the summit of a mountain, and Stiperstones and the Wrekin, although not that lofty, make a very good place to start. If you mark the occasion with a special treat and a photograph for the family album, you could maybe pave the way for a future in more ambitious mountain climbing! Other projects include trying to find fossils on Wenlock Edge, orienteering controls in Haughmond Forest, or engravings of lost Iron Age treasures at Bury Ditches. And if that still isn't enough, really questing minds can take up the 'Extra Challenge' that has been included with every walk. Usually it is a tally of five different items to spot along the way, and sharp eyes are needed. Even the adults can be enlisted to join in this one, but you may well find that the children are best!

So now you are ready to get started, and all the specific information you will need about each described route is set out at its beginning. It is impossible to be precise about the time you can expect to take because youngsters are natural dawdlers! So be prepared to linger; take snacks with you, call in where there is a shop, stop for a picnic or have a meal at the local pub. Whatever facilities are available have been listed. Hopefully 'going for a walk' will magically become an exciting prospect for the whole family. Good luck on your journeys!

Judy Smith

ACKNOWLEDGEMENTS

My thanks go to Eric for his unfailing support – and, of course, to the real stars of this book, Sam, Tom, Anna, James, Freddie, Ben, Becky, Jocelyn and Amber.

Llanymynech Rocks

A Walk Set in Stone

Relics from Llanymynech's industrial past scatter the route

This is a truly exceptional walk, fascinating from the moment you set off. The area known as Llanymynech Rocks was quarried for its limestone until the 1930s. Now the vegetation has grown over, it is a delightful nature reserve with seasonal wild flowers and butterflies in plenty. The path taken here follows the story of the stone, leaving the quarry down a steep tramway to reach the huge restored kiln in the valley below. The placards along the route are clear and interesting, so children will have no difficulty imagining the heavy loaded trucks being winched down the hill, and what it was like to work in the heat of the huge furnace. The lime was eventually taken away by rail or canal. Sadly neither is operational now, but the canal is being restored, and there is plenty for the children to see on the final section along its towpath.

Llanymynech Rocks

 **Getting there**
Llanymynech lies on the A483 between Oswestry and Welshpool. Head north from the village for 1 mile and turn left at Pant, following the brown sign to 'Llanymynech Rock'.

Length of walk 2½ miles.
Time Allow 1½ hours.
Terrain Clear paths with a steepish descent down the old tramway. Only the Heritage Area is suitable for pushchairs (the car park for this is signed off the A483 in Llanymynech).

The Walk

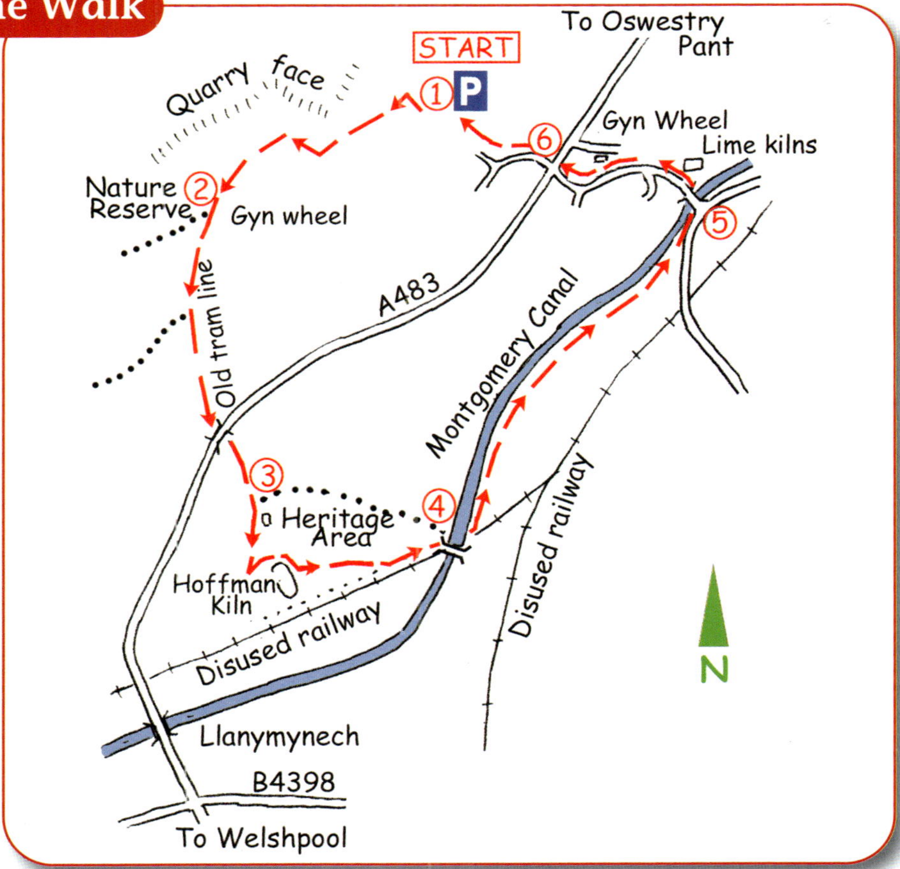

Quarry face

START
① P

To Oswestry
Pant

⑥ Gyn Wheel
Lime kilns

Nature
Reserve ② Gyn wheel

⑤

Old tram line

A483

Montgomery Canal

③ To Heritage
Area

④

Disused railway

Hoffman
Kiln

Disused railway

N

Llanymynech

B4398

To Welshpool

Kiddiwalks in Shropshire

Start/Parking The free car park at the end of the rough track at the top of Underhill Lane (GR: SJ 271219).
Map OS Explorer 240 Oswestry.
Refreshments A further 200 yards up the A483, the Cross Guns Inn is child-friendly with an outdoor playground. Otherwise, Llanymynech has plenty of facilities.

1 Leave the car park through the metal kissing gate and keep uphill on the main track, ignoring all others. After passing through some jungly vegetation, the towering rock face is straight ahead of you. The section on the right is used for climbing and abseiling, so there may be some activity to watch. The path bends left to reach a junction beside a huge drum, known as a 'gyn wheel'.

2 The wheel was used to lower loaded trucks down the slope while returning empty ones. Turn left and walk down the route of this tramway to the bottom. The path passes through a tunnel under the main road to enter the Heritage Area.

3 Keep right at the path junction here and after about 100 yards turn left, following

I can do that, too!

signs to the 'Hoffman kiln avoiding steps'. The enormous kiln is very impressive and you can walk all round it. When ready to leave, go through a gate at the side of the kiln and walk down the track, then straight on across the field.

4 At the end, go down steps to cross the bridge over the canal. Turn left along the towpath.

5 At the next bridge, leave the canal, cross the bridge and walk up the lane, passing lime kilns on

◆ Fun Things to See and Do ◆

There is so much interesting **wildlife** in the quarry. In late spring, the orchids are something very special and there are lots of magically-coloured butterflies all summer. The rock itself is limestone, formed when this land was under the sea some 340 million years ago. Limestone is actually the compressed fossilised remains of tiny sea creatures. How many billions are in that huge rock face?

The children can easily think themselves into **the role of a quarry worker** – there are lots of metal figures around to help the imagination. Information panels tell how the 'powder monkeys' scaled the cliffs carrying dynamite, and how everyone ran for cover before the explosion. Afterwards the men would break the rocks with heavy hammers and load them onto trucks, which was hard work. Boys were sometimes given the task of controlling the gyn wheel and they had to concentrate hard or the heavy trucks would hurtle down the hill and crash. Perhaps those who worked on the kiln had the hardest life. Can you feel how hot it must have been? They often got burnt, either with the fire or with the lime itself. One of the boards suggests you look for some of the coals these men may have dropped on the way to stoke the fire – can the children find any?

On the way back along the canal there are **birds and squirrels** and lots of farm animals to spot. Are there any unusual ones?

There's so much to see on this walk that you probably won't have time for the **Extra Challenge**! But just in case you do, can the children spot **a metal shovel, a round sign with five stars on it, an alpaca** (ask an adult …), **a cottage with the name of a season, an orienteering control** (half red, half white square – see Walk 9)? Anyone who finds them all is definitely as sharp as a needle!

Kiddiwalks in Shropshire

the right. At the top is the main road.

6 A few yards to the right of you is Gyn Lane, with another gyn wheel used for lowering trucks down this slope.
Cross the A483 carefully to return up Underhill Lane to the car park.

◆ Background Notes ◆

The **rock face** is impressive, and provides a nesting site for swifts, jackdaws and even peregrine falcons. Fallen stones frequently display fossils, but it is not a good idea to venture near the cliffs to search for them. **Orchids**, some rare, are the reserve's special treasure, but there are plenty of other wild flowers here.

The **story of the limestone** is clearly told on display boards. Lime was used as an agricultural fertiliser and also for building work – it was much in demand by nearby industrial Coalbrookdale. The Hoffman kiln was built rather late in the day (1899), making use of sidings from the Cambrian Railway to deliver coal. Sadly at this time Portland cement was taking over the role of lime mortar in the construction industry and the kiln closed in 1914.

The canal on this walk was originally known as the **Llanymynech Branch of the Ellesmere Canal**. Later extended south, the transportation of lime was its prime purpose. Originally profitable, the canal failed during the First World War, and after a major breach occurred in 1936, it was abandoned. Today, as the Montgomery Canal, it is gradually being restored to accommodate leisure boaters.

Selattyn Tower

Or Sleeping Beauty's Castle?

Exploring Selattyn Tower

Why would anyone build a tower on Selattyn Hill? No one really knows, but it may well be that the owner of the land at that time thought it would be a splendid place to sit and look out proudly over his domain. Long after he was gone, a forest was planted around that tower, and like Sleeping Beauty's Castle, it lay forgotten and hidden for many years. When the forest was felled recently the tower was revealed again – unfortunately with no slumbering princess inside! But once more you can share its most magnificent view, and the children might even enjoy picking out some of the distant landmarks with a pair of binoculars.

Aside from the tower and its views, this is a great walk in its own right, setting out on an attractive section of the Offa's Dyke National Trail. You are quite likely to meet some serious walkers here, and you can always pretend that you too are striding out for Chepstow, just a hundred or so miles away. It's going to take you at least ten days ... Maybe the children will be inspired for the future!

Kiddiwalks in Shropshire

2

Getting there *From Oswestry, head north on the B4579 towards Glynceiriog. Pass through the village of Selattyn and continue for a further 2 miles to a parking area under the rocks.*

Length of walk 2½ miles.
Time Allow 1½ hours.
Terrain Rough tracks and field paths – not suitable for pushchairs. Minor road at the end of the walk is quiet but, of course, take care.
Start/Parking The free parking area at Craignant (GR: SJ 254350).
Map OS Explorer 240 Oswestry.
Refreshments The car park has a couple of picnic tables. The nearest pub is the homely Cross Keys in Selattyn.

The Walk

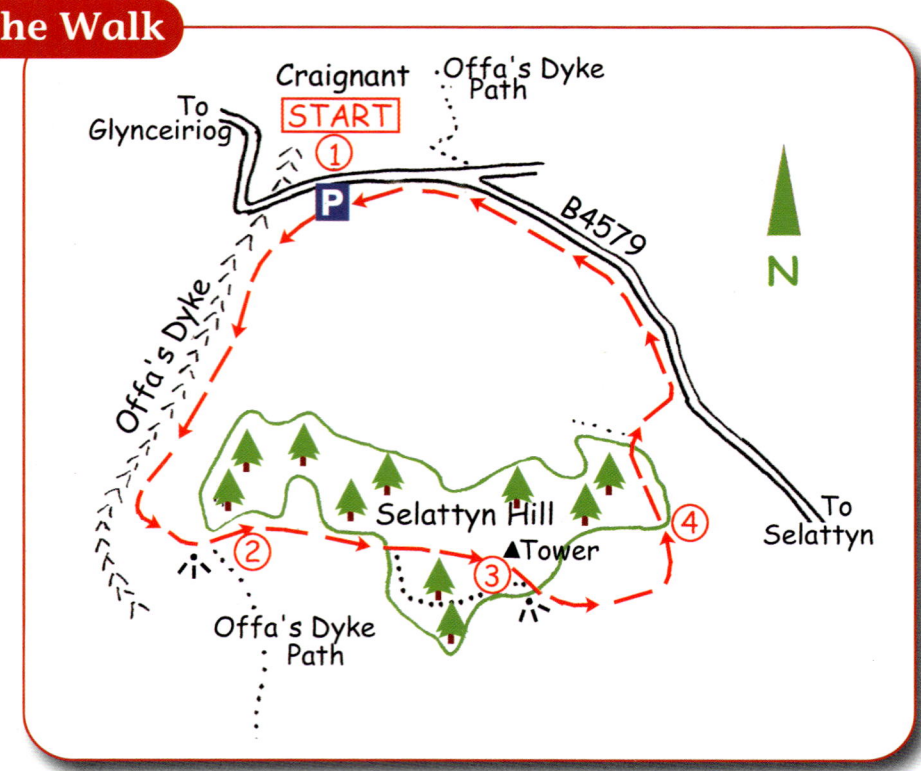

1 Leaving the car park, turn right. In about 150 yards, turn right up a track with an Offa's Dyke Path sign. The hard-surfaced track climbs steadily uphill. Where it swings left, keep ahead, following the 'acorn' signs that mark this (and all) National Trails. The path now passes between moss-covered stone banks and then comes out into a field. Here it bends left around the field corner and climbs to reach a prominent wooden signpost.

2 The Offa's Dyke Path turns right along the field edge here, but you leave it to keep ahead along the edge of the now-felled woodland. Continue to a gate in

◆ Fun Things to See and Do ◆

The **Offa's Dyke Path** is a great long-distance route! Lots of people walk the whole 180 miles at a go (it takes about 2 weeks), carrying everything they need with them and staying in farmhouses and inns along the way. Would the children like to do that? What would they put in their rucksacks? A few spare clothes, pyjamas, toothbrush, hairbrush, money, sandwiches for lunch each day – what else? It isn't fun if the rucksack is too heavy, so they have to think carefully what they really, really need. If you meet some walkers, the children could ask them how far they are going – and how heavy their sacks are! If everyone's keen, maybe you could plan some future less-ambitious escapade, perhaps with a one-night stop.

The stumps of trees around the tower show how thick the woodland here once was. Can the children remember **the story of Sleeping Beauty?**

On the way down, look out at the view. To make sure everyone looks hard, here is the **Extra Challenge** – between leaving the tower and reaching the car park, can the children spot **a smoking factory chimney, a church tower, a picture of a wren, a red dragon** and **a blackbird**? Anyone who gets all those is truly as sharp as a razor!

the angle of the woodland, from where an obvious path ahead leads to Selattyn Tower.

3 From the tower a narrow track heads downhill to the information panel telling its story. Take the little path opposite this panel, which leads to a seat with splendid views. Cross the nearby stile and walk downhill through the field to cross another stile on the far side. Continue descending with the wall on your right, cross a stile near a ruined building, and carry on downhill. At the bottom of this field turn sharp left (there is a signpost), and again with a wall on your right, walk towards the wood.

4 A stile takes you onto a path skirting the lower edge of the wood. Reaching a hard-surfaced track, turn right and descend again. At the road turn left for something like ½ mile to reach the car park.

◆ Background Notes ◆

Selattyn Hill stands on the line of **Offa's Dyke**, the 8th-century earth barrier built by King Offa of Mercia to separate and defend his land from the Welsh tribes to the west. It stretches some 180 miles between Prestatyn and Chepstow. The B4579 passes through Offa's Dyke just beyond the car park. On the walk, the best view is from the signpost at the top of the hill (point 2).

Selattyn Tower was built in 1847, but nobody is quite sure why. There were no trees on the hill then, and it was probably just a decorative 'folly', a place to sit and enjoy the view – and maybe it also provided cover for grouse shooting. In the Second World War it was used as a lookout post by the Home Guard, who installed a large gun here. The tower actually stands on the site of a Bronze Age cairn and you can still see the ring of stones surrounding it.

The view you have coming down the hill is to the west, with the isolated hump of the **Wrekin** right of centre. **Caer Caradoc**, the **Long Mynd** and the other Shropshire hills are to its right, while the Welsh hills are to the left.

3

Ellesmere

'Messing about in boats'

Feeding the geese at the Mere

The Mere at Ellesmere is a delightful place for young children. The multitude of ducks, geese and swans know just how to present themselves courteously to the visitors, and get invited to join in any picnic that's going. It has to be said that so much bread and cake is not exactly good for their health, and authentic duck food, on sale at the visitor centre, is definitely preferable!

You may well have to prise the youngsters away from the fun at the Mere, but older children will enjoy going on through the town to the old canal wharf with its crane and former warehouse still standing. There are always narrowboats moored along this 'Town Arm' and maybe there will be someone happy to chat to you about life on board. Beyond the Town Arm, the main canal is very popular, and should be fairly buzzing with boats at the height of summer. You might be tempted to walk on to watch them manoeuvring at Ellesmere Tunnel before you make your way back over the hill to the Mere.

Kiddiwalks in Shropshire

3

Getting there *Ellesmere is 16 miles north-west of Shrewsbury. The Mere is on the Shrewsbury road (A528) out of town.*

Length of walk 2 miles.
Time Allow an hour or more.
Terrain Pavements, hard-surfaced towpath and a firm earth track over the hill at the end. Suitable for all-terrain pushchairs.
Start/Parking The Meres visitor centre (GR: SJ 406346). There is roadside parking at the Mere, otherwise at Castlefields (opposite) for a small charge.

Map OS Explorers 240 Oswestry and 241 Shrewsbury.
Refreshments Snack kiosk and The Boathouse restaurant beside the Mere.

1 With the Mere and visitor centre on your right, walk up the road into town. Pass the church, then take the first road left after the garage (Watergate Street). At the first road junction bear right, and soon bear left along Scotland Street.

2 Turn left into Wharf Road to reach the wharf. Join the towpath and walk up to the top of the Town Arm.

The Walk

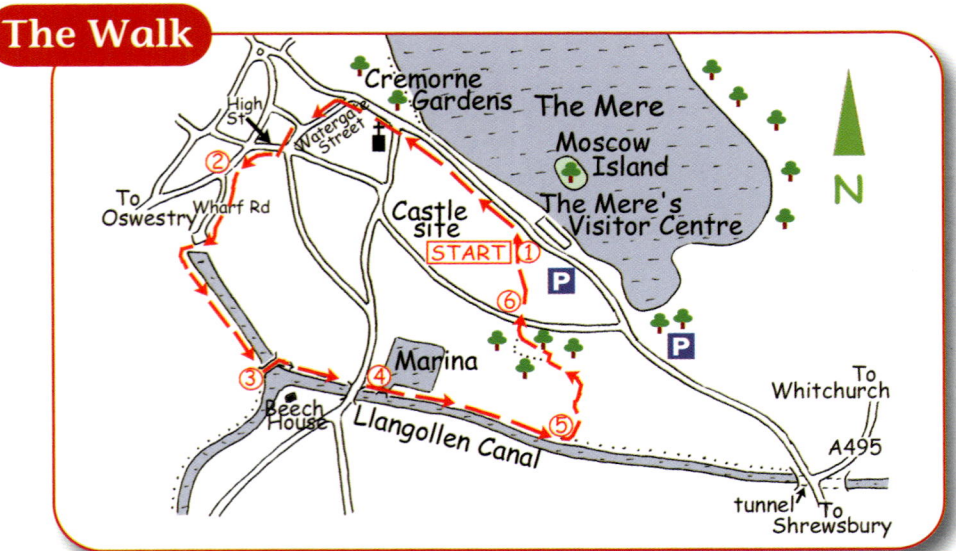

3 Turn left over the wrought iron bridge and continue along the towpath, passing under the road bridge.

4 A footbridge takes you over the entrance to the marina. Carry on along the towpath for another 400 yards or so to where a sculptured bollard stands beside the path.

◆ Fun Things to See and Do ◆

Everyone will enjoy **feeding the amazingly-bold ducks, geese and swans** at the Mere. Make sure that you go into the **visitor centre**, where there is plenty of interesting wildlife information and, in springtime, a camera relaying pictures of the herons' nests on Moscow Island. In summer it is possible to hire rowing boats on the Mere, or take a trip out in a genuine steamboat.

On the canal, **the boats are fascinating**. You can get a close look at some as you walk beside the Town Arm. Later on you get a good view of the marina when you cross the bridge over its entrance. How many boats are in there? (The answer is about 100 when it is full.) Look out for boats with traditional 'roses and castles' painting on the doors or on the pots and pans on top. Around 200 years ago, before the railways and when roads were not good, narrowboats like these were used to carry heavy goods like coal and lime around the country. The boatman would live in a little cabin at the back of the boat, and very often his wife and children would live there too. The cabin had to be small because all the space was needed for cargo, so if there were a lot of children in the family, they had to take turns to go to bed while the others helped with the boat!

And now for the **Extra Challenge**. While taking this walk, look out for – **a swan, a house with the name (and picture) of a duck, the number 58, a boat with a dog on board** and **a Victorian post box** (it has the initials VR). Did anyone spot them all? They have Super-vision!

Kiddiwalks in Shropshire

3

5 If you want to see the tunnel, continue on the towpath for a further 500 yards or so. Otherwise, turn left here (there is a swan logo Circular Walk sign) and follow the path up into the wood. Now you must follow the swan signs – keep ahead, then turn right (don't go up the steps) and finally turn left. The path runs along the top of the ridge, and then drops down to a gate.

6 Cross the road. Castlefields

At the canal junction, with Beech House across the water

car park is on your right, but to return to the Mere follow the grassy track across the field.

◆ Background Notes ◆

The **Mere** is the largest of many such lakes in this area. They were formed when the last Ice Age glaciers retreated some 10,000 years ago. Debris dragged back at this time resulted in mounds known as moraines – the wooded hill you cross at the end of this walk is one of these.

The waterfront at the Mere continues into **Cremorne Gardens**, where there are abundant rhododendrons and some stately old trees. If the children are too young to manage the walk described here, you can simply carry on along the pushchair-friendly path that runs about halfway around the Mere.

The **Llangollen Canal** was originally known as the Ellesmere Canal. Its architect was Thomas Telford, and he drew up most of his plans in Beech House, the large brick edifice overlooking the junction with the Town Arm. The whole canal opened at the beginning of the 19th century and would have been abandoned after the Second World War if it had not provided the water supply for Crewe. Now it is the most popular stretch of leisure waterway in England.

Whixall Moss

Water, Water, Everywhere

One of the lakes at Whixall Moss

This is a walk on the wild side, along paths that are literally buzzing with wildlife. Depending on the season, curlews' cries haunt the air, snipe spring out from under your feet, butterflies dance, dragonflies hover, pond-skaters scurry across the water and you may even spot one of the enormous rare raft spiders. The added bonus on this walk is the stretch along the Llangollen Canal, which skirts the edge of the reserve. There are sure to be colourful narrowboats, and children will enjoy seeing their crews operating the big lift bridge near the car park.

The Moss is at its very best on a warm sunny day, when the wildlife turns out in force, and the paths underfoot are at their driest. This walk is not long (although you can easily extend it), so take your time, maybe bring along your binoculars, and keep your eyes and ears open!

Kiddiwalks in Shropshire

4

Getting there *Whixall Moss is midway between Whitchurch and Wem. From the A495 Ellesmere–Whitchurch road, turn off at Welshampton towards Wem and then turn left in Northwood, following brown signs to the NNR. After Dobson's Bridge, a similar sign points left to the car park.*

Length of walk 1½ miles. The extension would add a further mile.

Time Allow an hour for the main circuit.
Terrain Canal towpath, then peaty tracks (be prepared for some mud in wet weather).
Start/Parking Morris's Bridge free car park (GR: SJ 493354) – cross the lift bridge.
Map OS Explorer 241 Shrewsbury.
Refreshments There is a picnic area at Roundthorn Farm, about ½ mile down the towpath (you would pass it taking the extension walk). A little further on you could visit the delightful

The Walk

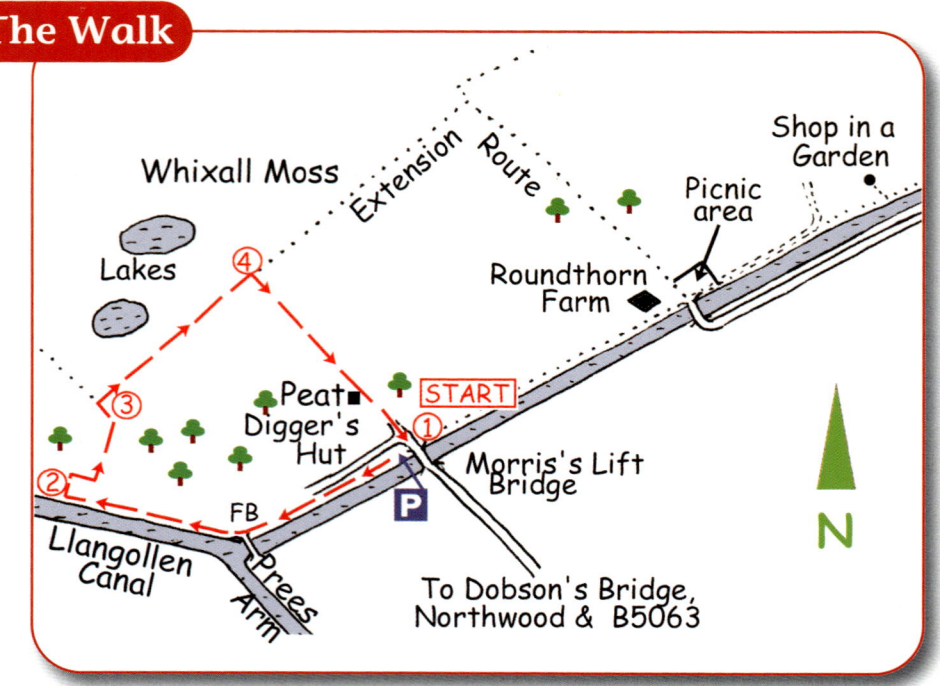

Whixall Moss

Extension Route

Shop in a Garden

Picnic area

Lakes

Roundthorn Farm

④

③

Peat Digger's Hut

START

①

Morris's Lift Bridge

②

FB

P

Llangollen Canal

Prees Arm

To Dobson's Bridge, Northwood & B5063

N

'Shop in a Garden', open in summertime to serve the boaters who moor outside. Or you could go back to Northwood where you will find the Horse and Jockey.

1 From the car park, walk up to the canal towpath and turn right. At the canal junction, bear right alongside the main canal (the Prees Arm on the left leads only to a marina). Continue for 400 yards.

2 Turn right down steps into the reserve. Continue ahead, turn right at the first junction (following a green arrow) on a track that soon bears left, and then go left again at the next junction, still following green. Keep ahead for 100 yards to yet another junction.

◆ Fun Things to See and Do ◆

A warm summer's day is by far the best for **wildlife**, when you can't miss the butterflies and dragonflies. Others to look out for are watervoles, kingfishers, curlews (more often heard than seen) and adders, who sometimes come out to bask in the sun. On the water you can see pond-skaters – and possibly a rare giant raft spider on the old peat diggings.

Right beside the car park is **Morris's Lift Bridge**, carrying traffic across the canal. Boaters must use an instrument called a windlass to wind up the heavy bridge before they can pass through the narrow section of canal beneath. Watch the bridge being lifted, then see if the person steering can get his boat through without touching the sides (or bumping his head!).

Finally that **Extra Challenge**. There's plenty to be found on this walk, but the challenge involves also spotting the following: **a pink arrow**, **a carving of a curlew**, **a dragonfly**, **a boat with roses and castles painting**, **bulrushes**. If anyone gets all five, they are sharp as a needle! And if you want an **Extra-Extra Challenge**, look out for the numbers **46**, **8**, **16**, **10**. Can anyone spot them all?

3 Turn right, again following green arrows. From this broad path you can see the big lakes on your left, and beyond them the flat landscape stretching to distant trees.

4 At the next junction (about 500 yards), follow the green arrows to the right to return to the car park. *If you want to extend the walk,* just keep ahead to the next junction (pink arrows) and turn right there, then right along the canal. On the main route there is a shed containing old peat-cutting equipment just beyond the gate – if you take the extension, you can always walk up from the car park to find it.

Background Notes

Most **peat bogs** in the UK were long ago drained for agricultural purposes – this one is a rare survivor. A moss forms from a glacial mere that has no outflow. Dead vegetation accumulates in its bed, eventually filling it, and in time this decomposing mass rises above the water to form a peat bog, colonised by acid-loving plants. In this strange environment, plants and animals are naturally preserved over centuries. From an area just beyond point 4, three Bronze Age bodies and an axe-head were recovered. Commercial peat digging ceased here some 20 years ago.

Vegetation and wildlife on the Moss are special. Sphagnum bogmoss and white cotton-sedge abound and there are rarities like bladderwort and the insect-eating sundew. You might like to look up other curiosities like four-spot chaser dragonflies and raft spiders before you set off. Warm days bring out the adders, who are shy creatures and will slide away if they hear your footfall. If you should see one basking beside the path you can admire its beautiful markings. And do not be afraid, it will not harm you unless molested.

When **the canal** was first built (1804) it had a bed of puddled clay and virtually floated across Whixall Moss. A gang of 'navvies' was employed full-time to raise the canal banks as they sank, until the installation of sheet steel piling in the 1960s.

5

Brown Moss Nature Reserve

'Down in the Forest Something Stirred'

Down by the water in Brown Moss

Brown Moss has atmosphere – and plenty to keep the children interested. For a start you need only venture a few yards from the car park to find trees that are perfect for young ones to climb, and a picnic table where everyone can have a snack while watching the ducks on the water. Beyond that there are the paths that wind through the woods and along the shores of the lake, crossing boggy areas on special boardwalks. Children can have fun looking for the wooden posts that lead you round on this walk (they aren't always that easy to spot) – and since it's only a mile long in total, even the shortest of legs should make it unaided to the end!

Kiddiwalks in Shropshire

5

Getting there *Brown Moss can be reached from the A41 north of Prees Heath. Approaching from Whitchurch, head south on the Wolverhampton road. At the second roundabout after leaving town (the first after leaving the by-pass), keep straight ahead and in about ¾ mile take an inconspicuously signed left turn into a narrow lane. At the junction in 500 yards branch left and continue for approximately 1 mile to a concealed parking area on the left.*

Length of walk 1 mile (and there is a short cut!).
Time Allow ¾ hour.
Terrain Wide paths, sometimes boggy in places. Not suitable for pushchairs.
Start/Parking The largest signed free parking area for Brown Moss (GR: SJ 563395).
Map OS Explorer 241 Shrewsbury.
Refreshments There is one picnic table at the car park. Alternatively, you will find all facilities in Whitchurch, 3 miles away.

1 Cross the shallow ditch beside the car park and bear right to the wooden seat at the top of the grassy clearing. Here a yellow-topped marker post points you left on a wide track into the wood.

2 Reaching white-and-black Beehive Cottage, turn left along the hedge and continue to a fork

◆ Background Notes ◆

A moss, like a mere, is glacial in origin. When the last glaciers retreated around 10,000 years ago, they dragged with them debris, and where pockets of ice remained in the debris, a mere was formed. A mere has a bed of clay, and since there is no stream running in or out of it, dead plant and animal matter is retained, finally filling it. Acid-loving plants then move in and thrive on this decomposing substrate to create a 'moss'. **Brown Moss** is a classic example, and has been designated a Local Nature Reserve and a Site of Special Scientific Interest. It is home to a wealth of interesting flora and fauna, with perhaps the most prized being the rare floating water-plantain and the great crested newt.

The Walk

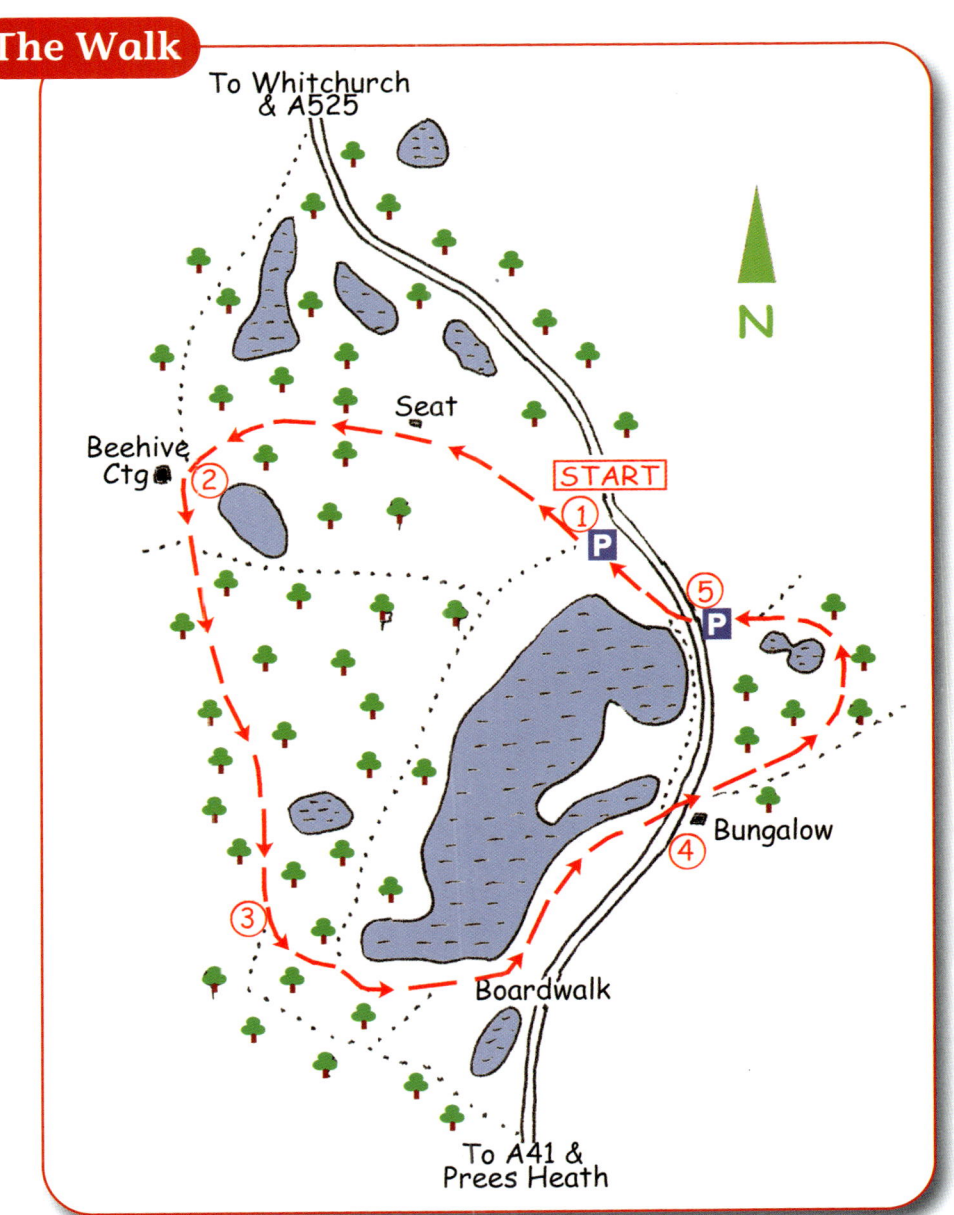

To Whitchurch & A525

N

Seat

Beehive Ctg

START

Bungalow

Boardwalk

To A41 & Prees Heath

Kiddiwalks in Shropshire

5

in the path. Bear left into the wood and keep straight ahead on a wide path until you cross a short boardwalk over a shallow ditch.

3 Immediately after the boardwalk turn left (look for the wooden marker post) and follow a more indistinct path through the trees. At the T-junction, with the lake ahead, turn right. Soon a long section of boardwalk carries you across the reedy area at the tip of the lake, after which the path continues along the shore and beside a long creek. At the tip of the creek, take a path on the right to reach the road in front of a bungalow.

4 Cross over to a path on the left of the bungalow, immediately forking left. The path winds through the trees, passing some beautiful overgrown lakes where dead branches give an eerie effect. Meeting another track, turn left and walk through the small car park to the road.

5 Cross and take the path opposite, which runs along the lake shore to your car park.

◆ Fun Things to See and Do ◆

This route is marked throughout by **wooden posts**, some of which have yellow-painted tops. Children can have fun running ahead to spot the posts, and they will need to look especially carefully at point 3 (after the boardwalk).

If you look in the shallow water margins and in the reeds you may see **frogs** and even **newts**. In spring there should be frogspawn. On a warm summer's day **dragonflies** and **damselflies** hover over the water.

And of course on a short walk like this there must be an **Extra Challenge**. Can anyone spot **a thistle, the date 2006, a brown butterfly, bulrushes** and **a moorhen**? A bonus is in order for **a bird's nesting box in a tree** and **a frog**. Well done!

Grinshill

Of Green Lizards and Red Stone

The view from Grinshill

Grinshill is a small hill with a king-sized view! It doesn't take long to climb, and with a very young family, maybe that is all you want to do – just sit on the top and treat yourselves to a picnic. Older children will enjoy the rest of this ramble, going over heathland and then down into the woods around the base of the hill. Here are the famous old Grinshill stone quarries, now overgrown and hung with lichens and ivy, a strange eerie world. Along with the red sandstone you can see Grinshill's unique white variety, its colour and nature changed by long ago volcanic activity. This white is in fact a creamy-beige colour and is very much prized for building stone. And the children might like to know that a little lizard-like dinosaur called the Rhynchosaurus roamed here around 200 million years ago. Fossilised bones and footprints have been found in the cut stone and even today quarry workers are told to keep their eyes open for more!

Kiddiwalks in Shropshire

Getting there *Grinshill is just south of Wem. Turn westwards off the A49 at Preston Brockhurst. After approximately ½ mile follow brown signs left to Corbet Wood.*

Length of walk 2½ miles.

Time Allow 1½ hours. Walking to the top of Grinshill takes about 15 minutes.
Terrain Woodland paths and tracks. Not really suitable for pushchairs. Children will need to be supervised on the summit of Grinshill because at one point there is a rocky

◆ Fun Things to See and Do ◆

At the top of Grinshill, older children could identify some of the distant hills, using the **toposcope**. It seems ridiculous that a hill of only 192 m (630 ft) should have the best view in Shropshire, but can you think of any better?

Down in the quarries, take a good look at the **Grinshill sandstone** because it really is famous building stone that has found its way into some high places. In Shrewsbury it was used for the library and for English Bridge among other places. Further afield – well, the Prime Minister sees quite a lot of it because it forms the door surrounds of 10 Downing Street.

The quarries themselves are interesting places to explore, with little paths winding through clumps of vegetation, and plenty of blocks of stone around. This could be a great place for **hide-and-seek** – although you might find it quite difficult to find the person hiding!

Finally, what about that **Extra Challenge**? On the walk, look for **some heather**, **a purple arrow**, **a bird table**, **a church tower** and **a jubilee seat** (whose jubilee would this have been?). The really keen-eyed ones might also like to look out for **the date 1852** and **a royal crown**. Anyone who spots all those really deserves the heartiest congratulations!

The Walk

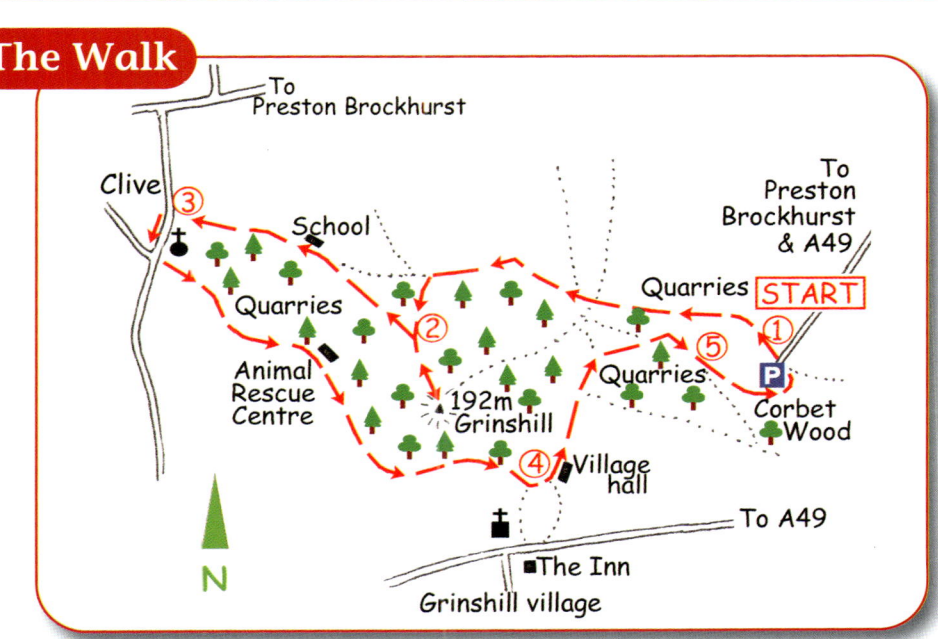

edge with a sheer drop.
Start/Parking The free parking area for Corbet Wood (GR: SJ 525238).
Map OS Explorer 241 Shrewsbury.
Refreshments None on the route, although there is an inn in Grinshill village. You could have a picnic on the hill itself or in Corbet Wood at the beginning or end of the walk. There are no tables in the parking area but just up the track into the wood you will find some flat topped rocks that might serve!

1 Leave the car park and turn left up the rough lane. Pass a few houses at a cross-tracks (note the local stone) and continue until you reach a metal barrier on the left. Go through the barrier and keep ahead on the uphill path.

2 Where this path meets a wider one, turn left to reach the summit of the hill. That view really is amazing – allow time to take it in and consult the toposcope before you return to the junction at point 2 again. This time carry on ahead until you reach a rough lane in front of the school. Turn left alongside the school wall. Ignore the heathland on your left and instead keep

Kiddiwalks in Shropshire

ahead on a sunken stone-floored track that comes out beside the church in Clive (note its two different local sandstones).

3 Turn left on the road, and immediately left again on a broad track. This soon passes more houses that once upon a time belonged to the quarrymen. Further on is the Animal Rescue Centre, after which the track descends towards the village of Grinshill.

4 At a junction on the edge of the village, turn left onto the track running behind the village hall. You are now on the route of the Shropshire Way. At the first junction go straight ahead into the wood on the uphill track. Stick with this track (losing the Shropshire Way) as it becomes sunken and bends to the right. Old quarries can be seen on both sides.

5 At a track junction, bear left on the sunken uphill track. This veers left and soon returns you to the car park.

◆ Background Notes ◆

Grinshill stone is a Triassic sandstone with high quartz content, particularly renowned for its durability and resistance to acid rain. Its value was known to the Romans who used it for buildings in Wroxeter (just east of Shrewsbury). Certain walls of that city are still intact today. The red colour of sandstone is caused by the grains of iron oxide that stick the sand particles together. Grinshill sandstone has been subjected to the high temperatures associated with volcanic activity, and has lost some of its colour while gaining in strength.

Before setting off, the children might like to find out what a **Rhynchosaurus** looked like. It was about 20 inches long and something like a green lizard, with a large head, a long tail and a sharp pointed bill to cut the plants it thrived on. In Shrewsbury town museum there is a reconstruction of a Rhynchosaurus, along with examples of bones and footprints.

Nesscliffe Hill

Haunt of the Highwayman

'Tea Tents' picnic area in the park

Children will love colourful Nesscliffe Hill. The red sandstone rocks are covered in green pine forest, and springtime adds a carpet of bright bluebells and then the purple of abundant rhododendrons. The woods are great to play in, but there is also an ancient hill fort to discover, and a lookout point where marks in the rocks were said to have been made by the cannons of Oliver Cromwell's men in the Civil War. Most exciting of all is a cave high in the cliff face, where a real highwayman and his horse lived for many years.

Kiddiwalks in Shropshire

7

Getting there *Nesscliffe is just off the A5, approximately 4 miles north-west of Shrewsbury. At the big roundabout on that road, turn right (signposted to Nesscliffe). Opposite the Old Three Pigeons Inn branch right, and continue for about ½ mile to a parking area on the right.*

Length of walk 1½ miles.
Time Allow 1½ hours.
Terrain Woodland paths, sometimes bumpy with tree roots. Some easy climbing at the start with a flight of downhill steps later. Not suitable for pushchairs.
Start/Parking The Oaks free car park, Hopton, Nesscliffe (GR: SJ 385199).

The Walk

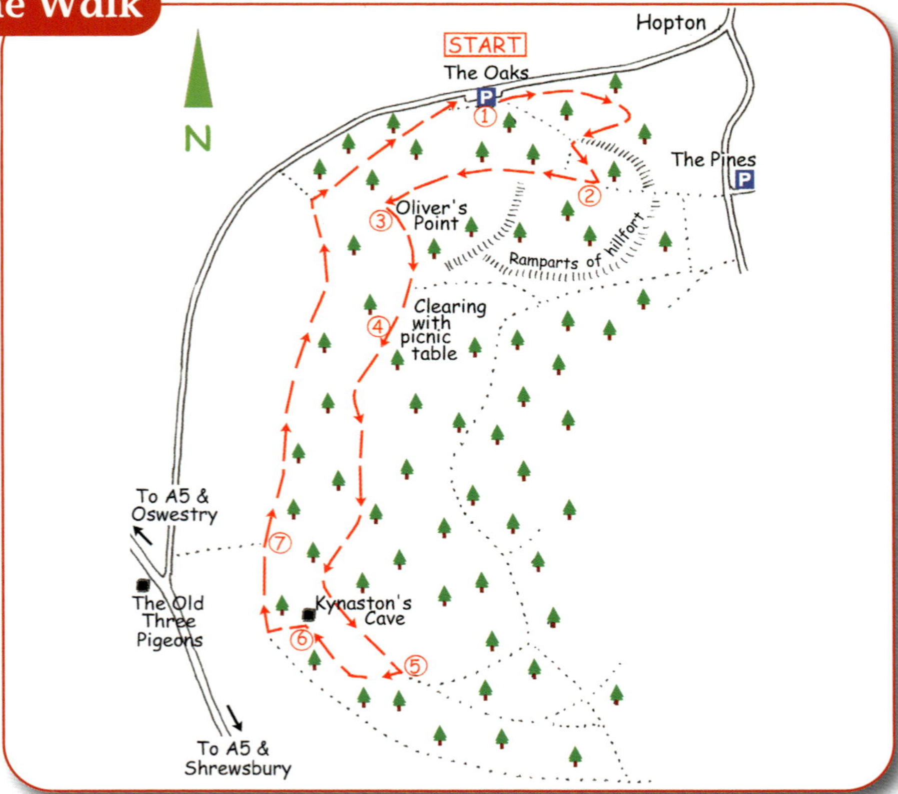

Hopton

START
The Oaks
①

The Pines
P

②

③ Oliver's
Point

Ramparts of hillfort

Clearing
with
④ picnic
table

To A5 &
Oswestry

⑦

The Old
Three
Pigeons

Kynaston's
Cave

⑥

⑤

To A5 &
Shrewsbury

N

Map OS Explorer 240 Oswestry.
Refreshments The Old Three
Pigeons is an ancient coaching
inn (1405) and the highwayman
Kynaston himself spent many a
happy hour there. Families are
welcome, the food is excellent,
and there is a small garden. Ask
them to show you Kynaston's
seat, taken from his cave (in the
fireplace).

1 From the car park, go into
Nesscliffe Country Park and turn
left on the uphill path. After
bending right, arrive at a path

◆ Fun Things to See and Do ◆

 **Pine cones** are plentiful and the children might like to collect some – perhaps to make Christmas decorations. What about a competition to see who can find the largest? And is it true that pine cones can predict the weather, the scales closing up for rain and opening out when it's fine? You could test it out.

The clearing known as the '**Tea Tents' area** has picnic tables where everyone could pause for a snack. There are also fallen logs to be climbed here, and of course it would make a great place to play hide-and-seek – provided limits were set, because that woodland stretches a long way!

The **double cave where Humphrey Kynaston and his horse once lived** is high up the cliff face, and the narrow steps leading up to it are now so worn that access would be dangerous. One just has to imagine what lies within – and however Humphrey managed to get his horse up and down those steps! Your youngsters might also like to know that a family with seven children lived here in the 18th century. Can they imagine that cave being their home?

For those who want an **Extra Challenge**, here are five items to be spotted on the walk – **a holly tree, a squirrel, a blue-painted horseshoe, a fallen tree** and **a tractor**. Anyone who sees them all can be sure that they have eyes like a hawk!

Kynaston's Cave

junction where you keep left (blue arrow).

2 Reaching a wooden signpost, turn right. The path now climbs through the ramparts of the hill fort. Near the summit, the path swings right to Oliver's Point. Look out to the volcanic Breidden Hills (can you see the pillar on top?) and spot the marks of Cromwell's cannons, but take care near the edge!

3 The path you now want starts beside the signpost and drops downhill through the rhododendrons to arrive at the 'Tea Tents' picnic area.

4 Cross the clearing directly to take the path on the far side (yellow arrow). This skirts the

fenced-off cliff edge to reach another signposted path junction.

5 Turn right to descend a long flight of steps with views of the old quarried cliff faces alongside. At the bottom, keep ahead beneath the cliff to find Kynaston's Cave.

6 From the cave bear left downhill, as indicated by the arrow, then turn right along the broad bridleway.

7 When you reach a junction where a sunken track goes left, continue ahead up the steps. Now simply follow the obvious track around the foot of the hill until you see a sign pointing left to The Oaks car park.

◆ Background Notes ◆

Nesscliffe Hill rises to a height of 150 m (480 ft). The hill fort near its summit was occupied from about 700 BC. Excavations in the 1950s revealed Roman pottery and coins.

Oliver's Point was apparently named after Oliver Cromwell, although there is no evidence that he ever went there. Quite possibly some of his men did, though, on their way to take Shrewsbury from the Royalists (1645). The round holes on the rocks at the point were reputedly made to anchor their cannons!

From the Point there are fine views across the Severn valley to the **Breidden Hills** in the south-west. They look like volcanoes and that is just what they were – the plunging contour of the last hill is due to quarrying for the hard volcanic basalt. Sharp eyes can pick out the pillar on top of this hill – it commemorates 18th-century Admiral Rodney, who distinguished himself in sea battles against the French and Spanish.

A century or so ago, the **flat clearing** was used for local festivities. Wooden 'tents' were put up, dances and tea parties were held here and there were competitions and even a maze to keep people amused.

Kynaston's Cave was indeed the residence of a highwayman. Humphrey Kynaston (1474–1534) was of noble birth but in his youth became something of a tearaway. Wanted for murder, he took refuge in the cave with his horse, Beelzebub. From here he began preying on the wealthy wool merchants returning along the Holyhead road with their profits from the London markets. Sharing his spoils with the local poor who fed him, he was regarded as a sort of 'Robin Hood', and his exploits became legendary. Beelzebub apparently had magical powers and one story has him vaulting the Severn at Montford Bridge to escape the sheriff's men. If you could climb up to the cave, you would see two rooms, one for Humphrey and one for his horse, with the initials HK engraved on the partition between.

Shrewsbury Battlefield

A Sky Black with Arrows

On the trail above the fishponds

This walk is all about imagination. Without it you have a gentle stroll through the fields on an easy path; with it you have all the ingredients of a medieval battle – men shouting, pennants streaming, pikestaffs clashing, arrows darkening the air. The Battle of Shrewsbury, a clash between King Henry IV and a rebel army under Harry Hotspur, was one of the bloodiest battles ever to take place on British soil. Maybe the adults will remember Shakespeare's account of it in *Henry IV Part I*.

A gravelled pathway now encircles Shrewsbury battlefield and there are three information panels to tell the story. More has been included in the text here, so everyone can picture it as they go round. And at the end of the walk you can return to nearby Battlefield Farm, where there is a small exhibition with 'Archie Sparrow' turning out some fascinating medieval facts for the children. The organic shop, fresh-food cafeteria and locally-made ice-cream should go down well, too!

Shrewsbury Battlefield

Getting there *Shrewsbury Battlefield is 3 miles north of Shrewsbury, beside the A49. Approaching from the south, turn left at the first roundabout after the A53 intersection (signposted to Battlefield church).*

Length of walk 1½ miles.

Time Allow at least an hour.
Terrain Hard-surfaced track over almost flat terrain. Suitable for pushchairs.
Start/Parking The free parking area at Battlefield Farm, off the access road to the church (GR: SJ 515175). There is alternative parking beside the church.

◆ Fun Things to See and Do ◆

Adults can help the children to **imagine the battle** as they go round the site – the inserts in the text will help. From the **exhibition**, you can get an idea of what the armies were wearing, handle the chainmail, and look at the pikestaffs.

If the **church** is open, go inside – there's a mock-up of the battle lines. Outside, look at the gargoyles under the eaves – one or two are medieval soldiers. And are there thousands of men buried beneath your feet?

In summertime, **special events** are staged on the site, including hands-on demonstrations by the 'Battlefield Bowmen', experts in the use of longbows.

The battlefield land actually belongs to the farm and you may see **cattle in the fields** or **tractors** working. The Shrewsbury–Crewe railway runs alongside and there are sometimes **goods trains** pulling long lines of loaded wagons.

And for the **Extra Challenge** – can the children spot **a holly bush, the date 1403, a train, a bench, a metal gate**? Anyone who gets them all will really have been keeping their eyes open!

8

The Walk

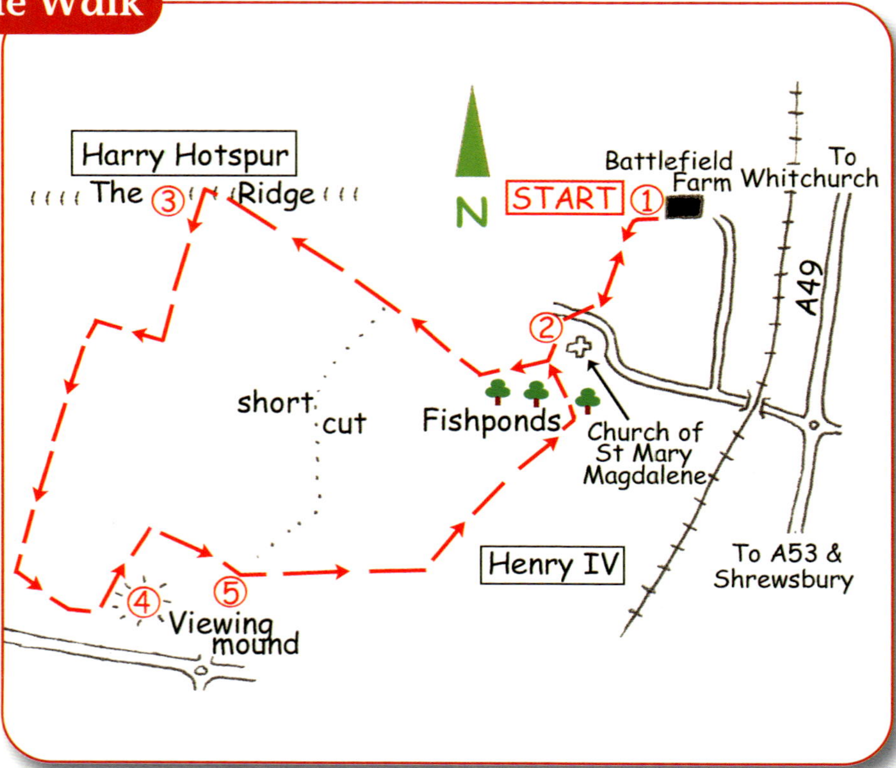

Harry Hotspur
The ③ Ridge
Battlefield Farm
To Whitchurch
START ①
N
A49
②
short cut
Fishponds
Church of St Mary Magdalene
Henry IV
To A53 & Shrewsbury
④ ⑤ Viewing mound

Map Explorer 241 Shrewsbury.
Refreshments Everything from ice-cream to a full breakfast or light lunch is available at Battlefield Farm throughout the year.

1 Leave the farm courtyard via the field gate and follow the path around the field edge. Cross the road to the church.

2 Cross the churchyard to leave by the far gate. Turn right on the track and continue to a path junction, just beyond a gate. The path left is a short cut, but you keep ahead here, climbing gently up the rise.

On this ridge Harry Hotspur massed his troops, archers in the front and everyone else behind. From here they looked down over the King's men –

and knew the battle was about to begin when the King's standard bearer walked out into the field.

3 Follow the path left downhill now; this hugs the field edges and finally turns sharp left to the viewing mound.

Climb up to the display panel and look over the fields to the church. What can you imagine? Hotspur's men are up there on the ridge, but the King seems to have about twice as many in the fields to the right. You can picture the battle right through from the first rain of arrows to the downhill charge of Hotspur's men. They were searching for the King but he had planted a few 'look-alikes' and they kept getting the wrong man!

4 Leaving the mound, take the path ahead along the field edge. It bends right to reach a junction.

5 The left path is the other end of the short cut. Ignore it and continue ahead across the field.

Here you are with the King's men, looking up at Hotspur's army on the hill. Their arrows are terrifying – the whole sky is dark with them and you know they can penetrate your armour. The hand-to-hand fighting is much less scary. Quite suddenly

The exhibition at Battlefields Farm is well worth a visit

the rebel troops start to run away. It's time to chase after them with your sword …

The path carries on beside a hedge and then on a walkway over a very boggy area in front of the church.

The pools beneath your feet are the remnants of fishponds installed after the college was set up (see Background Notes) – the chaplains needed a supply of fresh protein!

At the churchyard gate turn right to return the way you came.

Kiddiwalks in Shropshire

8

◆ Background Notes ◆

The **Battle of Shrewsbury** took place on 21st July 1403. Henry IV had seized the English throne from his cousin Richard II four years earlier, but his position was still unstable, and there had been many rebellions. The Percy family, who were his supporters, had repelled several attacks on the Scottish border. Unfortunately Henry hadn't honoured his promise of payment, and the ever-warmongering Percys became angry. Henry Percy (always called Harry Hotspur) and his uncle Thomas Percy gathered their armies and set out for the south, collecting more men along the way. Eventually they picked up the 'Cheshire Archers', the best longbow squad in the country. Owain Glyndwr had promised a Welsh force to join them, but they never arrived.

The King was heading for Scotland when he heard what was happening. He immediately turned west to meet the rebels. Harry Hotspur had established his position on a low ridge 3 miles north of Shrewsbury – the King, whose army was somewhat larger, had to make do with the flat fields below. Initially Henry offered terms, which Hotspur rejected. In mid-afternoon the battle began.

The archers in the front rank fired first. There were about 3,000 Cheshire Archers; they had the advantage of the hill and they could fire up to 12 arrows a minute. The King's archers were no match for them. At this point Harry Hotspur was decidedly winning – and he and his men made a mad charge down the hill, hoping to capture the King. It was badly judged, and in the hand-to hand fighting that followed, Harry Hotspur was killed. The rebels promptly lost heart and when the King's son, Prince Hal, mounted an attack from the rear they fled. After merely three hours around 3,000 men lay dead. They were buried where they fell, and three years later King Henry gave money to build the church over their grave, and installed a college of six chaplains to pray for their souls.

Henry IV was a Lancastrian (a son of John of Gaunt), and many people regard this battle as the first exchange of the English Civil War. Its other claim to fame is that though longbows had previously been used against the French, this was the first time that longbowmen had faced each other on English soil.

The Forest on Haughmond Hill

What's That Hiding in the Trees?

Follow the footprints and you won't go wrong

Forests have always been scenes of enchantment, places where fairies dance in the sunny glades and goblins peep from behind thick tree trunks. Think how many fairy tales are set in forests – there's *Little Red Riding Hood* for a start, and *Snow White and the Seven Dwarfs*, and *Babes in the Wood*, as well as latter-day *Where the Wild Things Are* and *The Gruffalo*. The forest on Haughmond Hill is not exactly a deep dark forest like some of those, but there will still be plenty to feed the imagination. And in this forest there is no fear of getting lost as all the routes are very clearly marked with little coloured footprints – the children can rush ahead and lead you round the trail, and if anyone gets tired, there's always a short cut nearby.

Kiddiwalks in Shropshire

🧭 **Getting there** *From the A49 east of Shrewsbury, turn onto the B5062, signposted to Haughmond Abbey. After passing the abbey take the next turn right. The car park is approximately 200 yards along on the right.*

Length of walk 2½ miles. Taking short cuts could reduce this considerably if you wish.
Time Allow 2 hours for the whole route.

Terrain Well-marked forest paths. The shortest marked circuit (approx ¾ mile) is suitable for pushchairs.
Start/Parking The free parking area for Haughmond Hill (GR: SJ 545147).
Map OS Explorer 241 Shrewsbury.
Refreshments Pine Tops Café is a mobile unit in the car park, open between 9.30 am and 3 pm (4 pm weekends) every day except Mondays and Tuesdays throughout the year. Hot and cold snacks, books and orienteering maps are on sale.

◆ Fun Things to See and Do ◆

Following the little **blue markers** through the forest is fun for everyone. Younger families might prefer to keep things short by taking the red route, or even the yellow, and other short cuts are obvious from the map.

In some areas the **trees** are mostly deciduous, in others, coniferous. Do the children know the difference?

And now for the **Extra Challenge**! Can the children identify **10 different trees** – or, at least, collect **10 different leaves** – on this walk? Suggestions are oak, beech, ash, hazel, sycamore, elder, silver birch, holly, Scots pine, Corsican pine, but there are plenty more. **Could anyone make it 15?** Even more difficult – can they spot **5 different birds**? (You can hear the birds all right, but they are hidden by those trees!) And if they can also find deer prints on the ground (cloven hoofs), they should award themselves a bonus – perhaps a special ice-cream!

The Walk

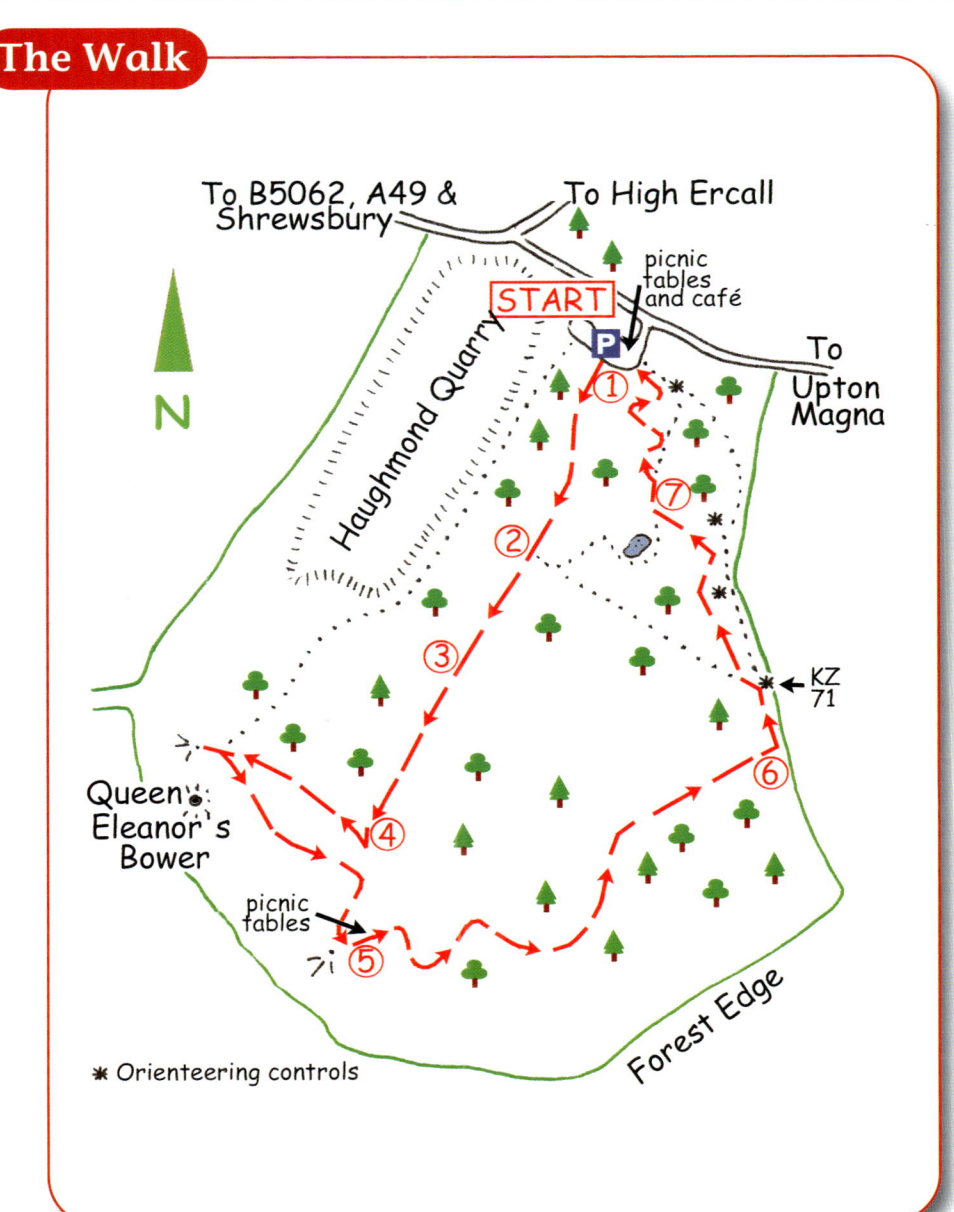

To B5062, A49 & Shrewsbury

To High Ercall

picnic tables and café

START

P

To Upton Magna

Haughmond Quarry

N

① ② ③ ④ ⑤ ⑥ ⑦

KZ 71

Queen Eleanor's Bower

picnic tables

Forest Edge

✳ Orienteering controls

The Pine Tops Café in the forest

1 Facing the 'Site Information' board in the car park, take the path immediately on the right. Very soon you pass a post bearing footprint logos for three separate walks. You will be following the longest 'blue' route – although there are short cuts. So keep straight ahead here until you reach a major path junction.

2 Here the yellow route – the 'all-ability-trail' – goes off left to pass an attractive pond on its way to rejoin the main route at point 7. Your *blue route* continues ahead, crossing an area of recently-felled trees to reach another junction.

3 This time the red route goes left. Your blue route continues ahead and eventually meets a broad cross track.

4 Turning right here (following *blue*) takes you to a magnificent grassy viewpoint overlooking Shrewsbury and the distant Shropshire Hills. *Blue markers* now return you to the broad track, from which a path soon leads right to another viewpoint, this time with picnic tables.

5 *Blue markers* now take you through stands of pine trees to rejoin the main track again. Turn right here, pass the point where the red route joins, and keep ahead to the forest edge.

6 Turn left here. Soon, as the main track bears left, you will see a post beside a path junction. The red and white square on it bears the letters KZ and the number 71. This is an orienteering control and there are 17 of them in total in the forest, most rather more hidden than this one. (There are actually 3 more you could hunt for between here and the car park – if you want to have a go, see the 'Background Notes' section.) About 100 yards after the orienteering post, take a lesser path on the right (waymarked red and *blue*).

7 At the junction with the yellow route, bear right and continue winding through the trees to return to the car park.

◆ Background Notes ◆

Haughmond Hill is managed by the Forestry Commission. The woods have been here a long time, and the viewpoint at point 4 is known to have been very popular with the Victorians. A painting shows them picnicking at the foot of a folly that once stood here. Beneath the viewpoint is a mound known as **'Queen Eleanor's Bower'**. Eleanor was the wife of Henry IV, and she is said to have watched the Battle of Shrewsbury from this point. Shakespeare refers to Haughmond as the 'bosky hill' behind which the sun rose on the battle day. Presumably there were woods here even in 1403!

Orienteering, a sport that originated in Norway, involves using a map to cross unknown terrain and find pre-set 'controls'. Permanent courses, like that at Haughmond, allow anyone to have a go at their leisure. Local and regional events use temporary courses intended to be navigated as quickly as possible and there are classes for all levels of experience. The easiest courses are for family groups and under-10s, so if you are inspired, you could follow it up on www.wrekinorienteers.co.uk – the website of the group who set this course. And if you want to do a bit more orienteering at Haughmond, three more controls are marked on the map here, but you might like to buy the special, more detailed map of the whole forest from Pine Tops Café.

Attingham Park

Dawdling with the Deer

Heading out from the deer park

The grounds of Attingham are full of adventure. Thick leaves to rustle in autumn, fallen logs to climb, and secret places to play hide-and-seek are there in plenty, but children will also love the River Tern winding through the woods, and the fun of crossing it on a wobbly wooden suspension bridge. Tucked in the forest glades are curious sculptures, and best of all there are the deer, who wander from the woods into acres of grassy meadowland. The walk takes you right through their park, so you should have no difficulty spotting them. This is a ramble packed with interest, and when you have finished, Attingham has a lot more activities in store specially for the children. You may well want to return …

Getting there *From the Shrewsbury by-pass take the Ironbridge road, the B4380. In the village of Atcham (1½ miles), cross the Severn and almost immediately turn left into the park.*

Length of walk 3 miles.

Time Allow 1½ to 2 hours.
Terrain Woodland paths and grassy field. Suitable for all-terrain pushchairs.
Start/Parking The car park for Attingham Park (GR: SJ 548100). There is a charge for entry to the grounds (National Trust members free). Grounds are open every day, 9 am to 5 pm in winter,

The Walk

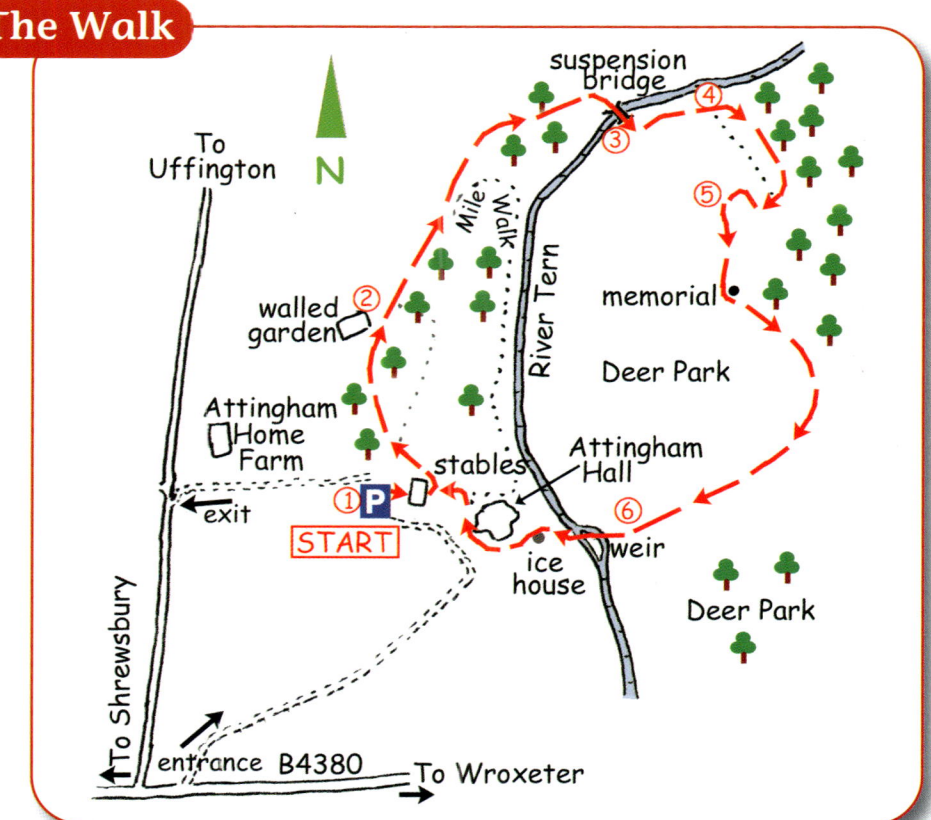

Kiddiwalks in Shropshire

10

9 am to 6 pm in summer.
Map OS Explorer 241 Shrewsbury.
Refreshments There are tearooms both at the stable-block entrance and in the mansion itself. Toilets are located in the mansion and at the walled garden (point 2).

◆ Fun Things to See and Do ◆

The highlight of this walk must be **the deer** so it is worth taking binoculars along to be sure of getting a good look at them. They are fallow deer – brown coloured with white spots – and the bucks (males) have large antlers, which they shed in the springtime. In the autumn rutting season you may see them fighting. The deer at Attingham are fed carrots, beet and deer nuts over the winter months and it may be possible to watch this if you check the time first. The **Family Activity Room** at point 2 has lots of information about the deer and about other special creatures like kingfishers and otters that inhabit the park.

In the woods are a number of **very old oak trees**, some dating back almost 500 years to the reign of King Henry VIII! Look out for one that has been dropping its dead branches and is now fenced off for safety.

There's plenty to see on this walk, but for those who need an **Extra Challenge**, look out for: **a tree guard** (fencing to keep the animals off), **a crown motif**, **a wood carving of a frog**, **someone with a black dog** and **an aged oak** (fenced off). If anyone manages to see all those, that really would be a superb effort. Well done!

As well as the playground and activity room, Attingham stages frequent **family events**, offers a child-orientated trail around the house and even runs a 'Tuesday Club' of activities in the school holidays. A further attraction is **Attingham Home Farm**, in the grounds. A traditional working establishment, it's worth a day's visit in itself!

The imposing Attingham Hall

1 From the car park, enter the grounds through the stables and immediately bear left. The walks are signed and you have only to follow the broad path through the trees to reach a walled garden. On either side of it are a children's play area and a picnic area.

2 The wide track continues to a junction. Keep to the left here, following the sign for the Deer Park Walk. Winding on through the woodland the path eventually swings right to cross a suspension bridge.

3 On the far side keep straight ahead, then turn left at a junction with a 'Woodland Walk' signpost. Soon you meet another signpost, which indicates the Woodland Walk in three directions.

4 Keep straight ahead here. The path bends right, climbs uphill past a pond, and bends right again. Continue past a very curious bird sculpture (what do the children make of it?), then almost immediately turn right to reach the entrance to the Deer Park.

5 Cross the Deer Park on the wide grassy ride, passing the Berwick Memorial. The deer could be anywhere, so keep your eyes open. Eventually a Deer Park Walk signpost directs you to the right to reach an exit gate.

6 After the gate, cross the stream on two separate bridges and then keep on the path passing the Ice House (peep inside) and then the front of the house. On the far side you can choose whether to go up the steps on the left or continue on the path to return to the stables and the car park.

◆ Background Notes ◆

Attingham Park is one of the grandest country houses in Shropshire. Set in 500 acres of parkland, it was built of Grinshill sandstone in 1785 to the designs of George Steuart, with later alterations being made by John Nash. Having passed through the hands of eight generations of the Berwick family, it is now in the care of the National Trust, and is still undergoing restoration. The 'trompe d'oeil' drawing room, ladies' boudoir, Nash picture gallery, kitchens and servants quarters are open to visitors and you can wander at will or opt for a tour taken by a costumed guide.

The **landscaped gardens** were created by Thomas Leggett and Humphry Repton. A much shorter 'Mile Walk' is an alternative here, although you don't get to see the deer. The lawns in front of the house and along the banks of the Tern are perfect for children's games and for picnicking.

11

The Wrekin

Feeling on Top of the World!

On the way to the Wrekin

There was once a giant with a grievance against the people of Shrewsbury and he set off with a shovelful of earth to dam the River Severn and flood the town. As he strode across the flat fields he met a cobbler carrying a bag of old shoes for repair and asked him how far he had yet to go. The cobbler, seeing what the giant had in mind, replied that it was so far that he had worn out all these shoes along the way – whereupon the giant angrily flung down the earth he carried, thus creating the Wrekin!

Whatever you may think of that story, the lonely hump of the Wrekin does have a magical air about it and you can't pass it without wanting to be up there. You can just tell it has a fantastic view! To the children it looks like a proper mountain, a real challenge they can't wait to take up. So chose a fine day, pack up a picnic, binoculars for the view, a camera to record the achievement and perhaps a few goodies for a reward at the summit. Off you go!

Kiddiwalks in Shropshire

11

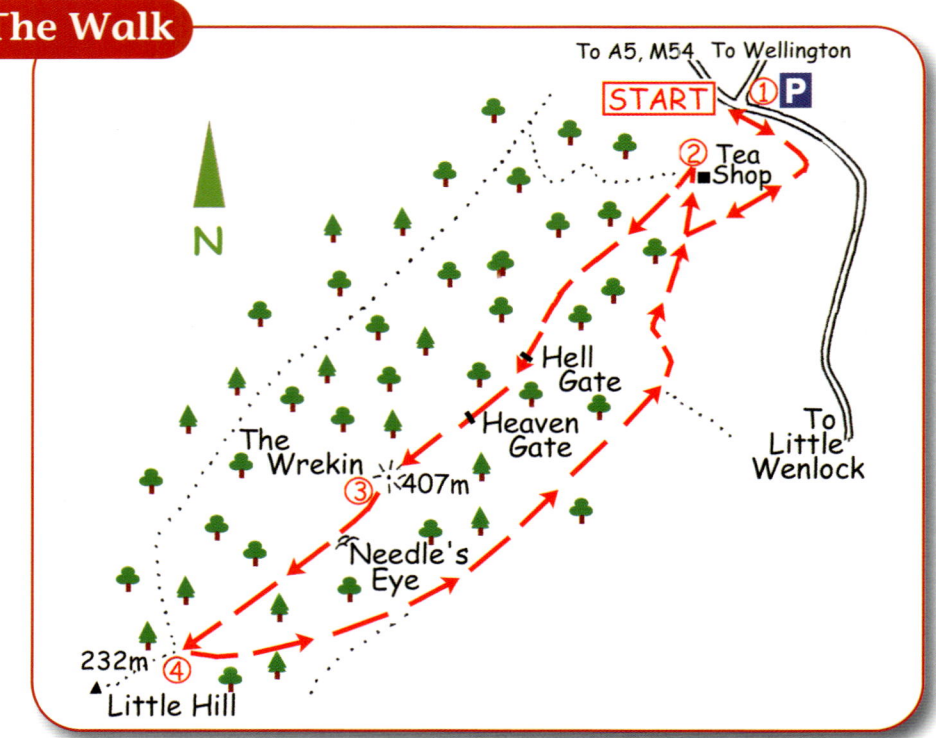

Getting there *Leave the A5/M54 at junction 7 and head south towards Little Wenlock. After about 1 mile (just beyond a road junction), the car park is on the left.*

Length of walk 1¼ miles to the summit. Whole circuit 3½ miles.
Time Approx 1 hour to summit. For the whole circuit allow 2½ hours.

Terrain A gradual sustained climb on a wide stony path. The descent is steep in parts, with an easy final section on forest track. The described way back is quite long, so younger families will probably find it better to return directly from the summit.
Start/Parking Forest Gate free car park, under the rocks on the Little Wenlock road (GR: SJ 638093).
Map OS Explorer 242 Telford,

The Walk

To A5, M54   To Wellington

START   ①🅿

② Tea
   ■ Shop

N

Hell
Gate

Heaven
Gate

The
Wrekin

③ 407m

To
Little
Wenlock

Needle's
Eye

232m ④
▲ Little Hill

Ironbridge & The Wrekin.
Refreshments A house on the way up doubles as a teashop on high days and holidays and has a toilet. Otherwise there is nothing on the route – but the Wrekin is a lovely place for a picnic!

1 From the car park, return to the road junction and cross the road to pick up the wide uphill track. After a couple of sharp bends to the right it reaches a house (the teashop) and then a barrier onto the mountain.

◆ Fun Things to See and Do ◆

As you climb the Wrekin **the view gets better and better**. This is how the world must look to the birds! Down below you can pick out farms and roads and animals grazing in the fields – and the four red towers of Coalbrookdale Power Station, and the winding River Severn. Take a long look at the **toposcope on the summit**. Older children can identify some of the hills – the long ridge of the Long Mynd, Stiperstones with jagged rocks on top, the abrupt bump of Caer Caradoc and Brown Clee with its radio mast, the highest point in Shropshire.

Scots pines grow near the summit on the way up. On the way down there are other coniferous trees. See how many different ones the children can spot (probably at least 5). You might need to take a small piece of each home to identify them.

For the **Extra Challenge**, look out for **a signpost saying, 'This Way', 'That Way' and 'The Other Way'**, **Coalbrookdale Power Station**, **the River Severn**, **a cairn of stones** (it's not at the summit!), **a pig on a picture**. Well done to anyone who gets them all! And as an Extra-Extra, who can spot some **deer**?

Finally, everyone must **celebrate a successful climb**! A 'summit pack' containing a few goodies (edible or otherwise) and perhaps a special drink could make future mountaineering a most acceptable project. And don't forget the photograph!

Walking down the main path

2 Turn left here and continue up the obvious broad track. In the 1st century AD a hill fort was established here, and the path passes through its two gates, inturned gaps between ramparts. At the summit a toposcope identifies all you can see.

3 Walk straight ahead across the summit to pick up a narrower descending track. Just after leaving, the rocks on the left contain the Needle's Eye (see Background Notes). Continue steeply downhill to arrive at a crosstracks where you can see a low hill ahead (aptly named Little Hill).

4 Turn left here on a path running through woodland around the flank of the hill. After about ½ mile it is joined by another track coming from below. Simply keep ahead with open fields now on your right to arrive eventually at the broad track on which you set out. Turn right to descend to the car park.

◆ Background Notes ◆

The **Wrekin** is composed of volcanic ash and lava, but it was never a volcano. It rises to only 407 m (1,335 ft) but looks much bigger because the land around is so low-lying. It isn't quite alone either. The Wrekin has a very little sister, the Ercall (pronounced Arcal) alongside and from this route you can see the old quarries on the Ercall. The two-tone pink and grey rock is particularly interesting to geologists.

The **Wrekin's summit**, like so many others in Shropshire, shows the presence of an **Iron Age hill fort**. Quite possibly this one was the capital of the Cornovii, and a tribal meeting place. In climbing you pass through the two fort entrances that are gaps in the ramparts – the outer is Hell Gate, the inner (narrower!) Heaven Gate. The view from the summit on a clear day is said to encompass 17 counties. The 'Beacon on the Wrekin', lit up at night, is a transmitting station used for telecommunications and broadcasting.

The rocks on the left just beyond the summit contain a slit known as the **Needle's Eye**. Legend has it that it was made by warring giants wielding a spade! It is said that to consider yourself a true Salopian, you must have passed through the Eye – but don't even think of trying it with the children!

This whole area was once a **Norman hunting forest** and today there are still large herds of fallow deer roaming the woods. Tiny non-native muntjacs have joined them.

Telford Town Park

A Surprisingly Rural Ramble

The colourful playground in Telford

Why on earth would anybody want to go for a walk in a park right beside a busy shopping centre at the heart of a big built-up area? Well, if you don't try it you'll never know! Telford Town Park was the inspired creation of the 1970s' planners, a long swathe of meadows, lakes, woodland and heath that stretches almost 2 miles from the town centre itself and where it is possible to feel as off-the-beaten-track as you might on any countryside walk. The route described here is really a grand tour of the park, but because so many short cuts are possible, you can easily adapt it to your own requirements. And if the youngsters want to divert to exploring little lakeside trails or tracking through the woods instead, that's fine too – they can't get lost, and they'll be just as tired at the end of the day. Of course, if they're not, there's always the adventure playground – and the boating lake …

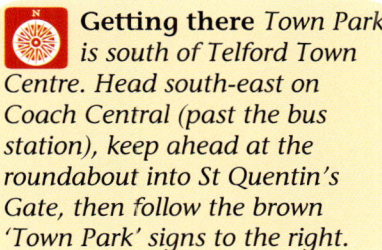 **Getting there** *Town Park is south of Telford Town Centre. Head south-east on Coach Central (past the bus station), keep ahead at the roundabout into St Quentin's Gate, then follow the brown 'Town Park' signs to the right.*

Length of walk 3 miles – but many short cuts are possible.

Time Allow 2 hours.
Terrain Mostly hard-surfaced tracks suitable for all-terrain pushchairs (earth tracks near the folly can easily be by-passed).
Start/Parking Pay and display parking at the main entrance, close to all facilities (GR: SJ 701085). Alternatively, there is a free parking area near point 2 (for this, continue down St Quentin's Gate, at the next

◆ Fun Things to See and Do ◆

 As you walk you will see many, many lesser paths, and you might choose to go **exploring round Randlay Pool and Blue Pool** or to go off into the **lovely wild meadow** near point 3. The heathland in point 4 offers lots of scope for **running up and down grassy banks**, and the flat 'arena' near the start is great for **ball games**.

So much woodland means that there are **lots of birds**. See how many different ones the children can spot as they go round. In the pools they may see **fish and frogs**, and even frogspawn in springtime. In summer there are lots of **dragonflies and damselflies** too, and long-legged **pond-skaters** on the surface of the water. The park is especially proud of its **rare spotted orchids**, at their best in early summer. Look for the purple flower spikes down by the Blue Pool or in the wild meadow.

For those who want even more things to spot, here is the **Extra Challenge**. Can the children find: **a red and white toadstool** (yes, it's there all the time!), **someone fishing, the words 'Rest after Work', a person wearing a hat** and **a mallard**? Anyone who did certainly had their wits about them!

The Walk

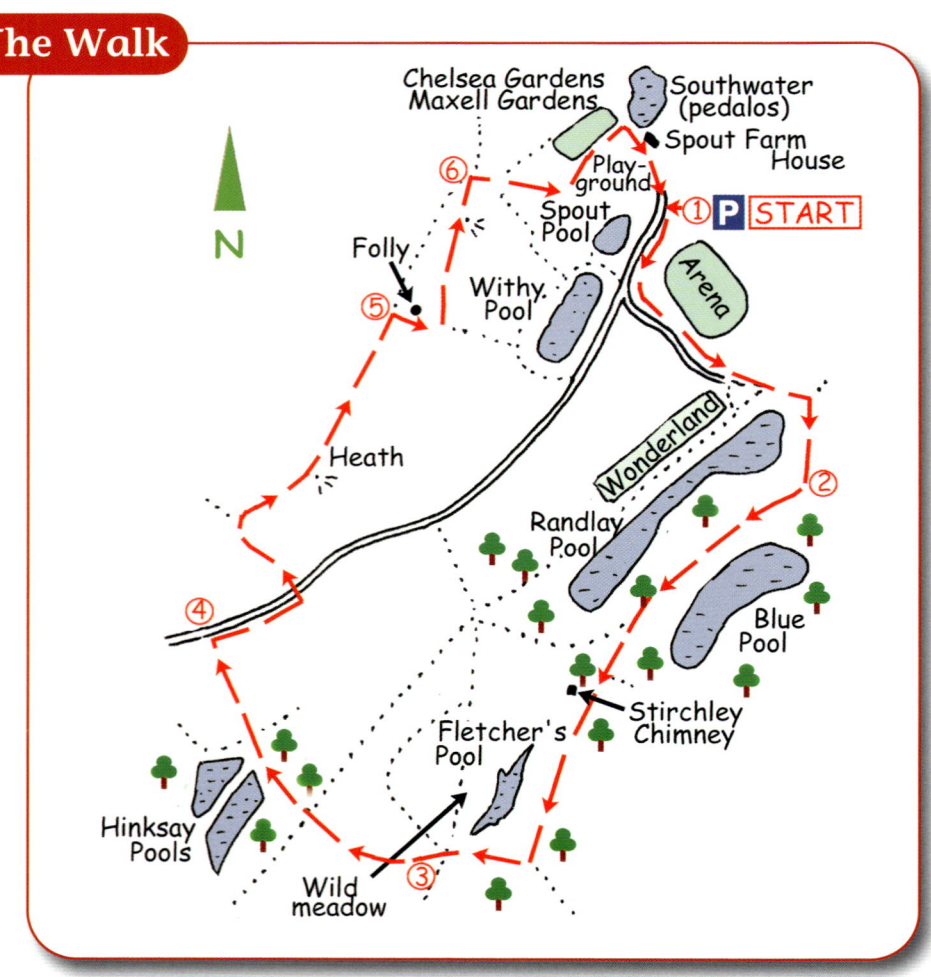

roundabout follow signs for Stirchley, take next right into Randlay Avenue and the car park is on the corner – GR: SJ 704078) **Map** OS Explorer 242 Telford, Ironbridge & The Wrekin. **Refreshments** Near the entrance,

Spout Farm House is both Information Centre and café, serving sandwiches, snacks and drinks.

1 From the corner of the car park, walk uphill into the park.

What is that I spy in the gardens?

When you reach a metalled road, Spout Farm House and the playgrounds are to your right. However, turn left and at the first junction, turn left again, following an arrow to 'Wonderland'. Continue downhill, bearing left at the entrance to Wonderland. Ignore a track going off right, and keep ahead round the end of Randlay Pool, the largest of the lakes.

2 Here a track from the free car park joins. Keep ahead, passing Blue Pool on your left. At the end of the pool, fork left, now skirting the edge of the park through woodland. Pass lofty Stirchley Chimney and continue to a T-junction. Turn right and carry on to a multiple junction where another pool and adjacent wild flower meadow lie to your right.

3 Turning right here would take you back towards Spout Farm. To continue with the walk, take the second path on the left, bending uphill to reach a junction with another metalled track. Cross directly and take the rougher track uphill, passing two fishing lakes. At the little car park, continue ahead to meet a road.

4 Turn right on the little road going into the park; this passes right through the park and could serve as another short cut. To continue with the full circuit, take the first track on the left, just past a house. At a fork, bear right, climbing up through the trees to open heathland with gorse and heather. You are high here, and there are views to the south-east towards Wolverhampton. Eventually the path reaches a fork where it seems a castle (actually a folly) is peeping over the trees ahead.

5 Turn right, and then keep left around the folly. An earth track now climbs through the trees to a high point with a toposcope. Again views are to the east – trees block off the Shropshire Hills on the opposite side. Continue along the path to another junction.

6 Turn right down the steps and you can see the playground ahead. To its left are ornamental gardens, and behind are Spout Farm House and the pedalo lake. Pass them all to return to your car park.

◆ Background Notes ◆

Telford Town Park was developed on the site of coal mines, brickworks and ironstone quarries that were abandoned in the mid-19th century. The different habitats in the park bear witness to their pasts – heathland on the acid soil of the former slag heaps, orchids growing in the more alkaline soils of the limestone quarries.

Stirchley Chimney, 203 ft high, was built by the Wellington Iron and Coal Company in 1873. It was never fired because the company went bankrupt soon afterwards. The Wrekin Chemical Company took it over, and used it to manufacture lime salts and naphtha charcoal – until the local residents complained of the smell!

Wonderland, near the beginning of the walk, is a theme park for the very young. Based on nursery rhymes and fairytales, there are lots of familiar characters to recognise, and access to the rides, maze and indoor play areas is happily included in the admission price.

13

Coalport

Strange Happenings in the Gorge

Where the Inclined Plain meets the canal

How can boats travel up and down hill? You can investigate that one at the beginning of this walk, and later on you can give some thought to the way natural bitumen might ooze from the walls of a brick tunnel. If it really fascinates you, you can put on a hard hat and go and see. Other features of this ramble in the Ironbridge Gorge are the huge bottle kilns of Coalport China, the great River Severn itself, and a pub that from its marked flood levels would seem to have spent a fair proportion of its life under water! Ironbridge Gorge is certainly a place of curiosities!

Novelty value aside, this is also a delightful walk along the banks of the Severn, and one that is very well endowed with pubs and picnic tables. So take your time, refresh yourselves, and maybe at the end of the day there will be time for a peek at the famous Iron Bridge, just a couple of miles upstream.

Kiddiwalks in Shropshire

13

Getting there *Coalport, south of Telford, can be reached from the A442 or the A4169. Approaching from Ironbridge, take the road east along the north bank of the Severn, following signs for the Coalport China Museum.*

Length of walk 3 miles.
Time Allow 2 hours.
Terrain Footpaths and hard-surfaced tracks. There is a long flight of steps at the beginning. Not suitable for pushchairs.

Start/Parking Just before reaching the China Museum, there is free parking on the roadside at the picnic site on the left (GR: SJ 695025). Otherwise there is pay and display parking at the museum itself.
Map OS Explorer 242 Telford, Ironbridge & The Wrekin.
Refreshments There are four pubs on the route, and picnic facilities at the start and halfway round.

1 From the free parking area, take the path up the left side of

The Walk

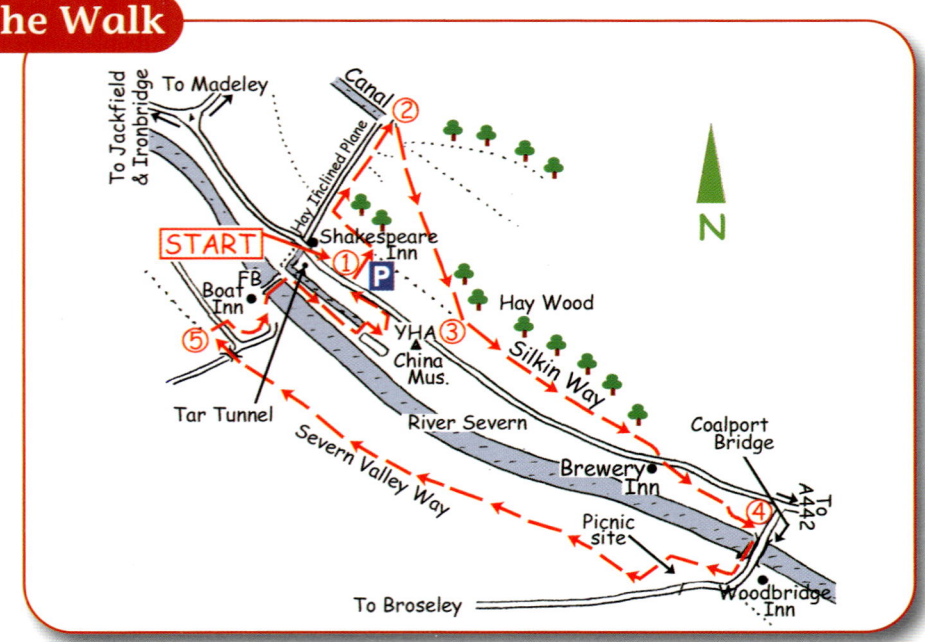

the picnic site. Reaching the track at the top (the Silkin Way), turn left. Immediately before the bridge, turn right to climb a series of steps alongside the Inclined Plane that carried the boats. Ignore all footpaths turning off right until you reach the top of the slope.

2 The path you need is the one on the right at the very top – but

you might like first to carry on a little further to get a better look at the top of the Inclined Plane and the canal that supplied it. When ready, take that path (signposted 'Coalport Bridge'), and at the fork in the field, bear right. A gate admits you to a path running down through Hay Wood.

3 Reaching the Silkin Way again, turn left and continue to

◆ Fun Things to See and Do ◆

It's a long climb up at the beginning, so you may need to do **a little step-counting** to help things along! Once at the top, imagination is needed because there is no water in this part of the **Shropshire Canal** now. But around 200 years ago, little square tub boats carrying coal or iron ore came along that canal, then went into a sort of cradle on wheels to be lowered down to the canal below. It seems very steep – they would have to be careful the cargo didn't spill out!

When you get to the Boat Inn take a good look at the door with all the **flood levels** marked. If there is heavy rain at the source in Wales, it is here in the Ironbridge Gorge that the water will rise most because the sides of the gorge are steep and there is nowhere for the water to escape. Would the water have been over anyone's head in January 2008?

And finally, just to keep everyone on their toes, here is the **Extra Challenge**. As you walk, the things to look out for are **a bird table, the date 1818, a picture of a kingfisher, the number 56** and **a lifebelt**. Anyone who gets them all is truly eagle-eyed!

its end. Go through the gate, cross the pub car park, and then the road to take a broad track opposite. It dips past some cottages, then bends right along the river bank to Coalport Bridge.

4 Cross the bridge, and take a track on the right signed to Preen's Eddy picnic site. Beyond the picnic tables, the path soon bends away from the river. Turn right on the broad track (the route of the Severn Way) and carry on through the woodland for about ¾ mile.

5 After crossing over a road, turn right, following blue Cycleway signs. Continue downhill, bearing left to reach the Boat Inn beside the river. Don't miss the flood levels marked on the black door! Now cross the footbridge. The old Coalport Canal is on the far side and you can see the bottom of the Inclined Plane under the bridge ahead. On the far side of the bridge (and canal) is a brick cottage and, beside it, the entrance to the Tar Tunnel. Whether you decide to visit that one or not, the canal towpath will quickly return you to the China Museum, with the roadside car park just to the left.

◆ Background Notes ◆

Hay Inclined Plane opened in 1792 and was in use for just over 100 years, until railway transport took over. The plane moved the boats through 205 ft – the equivalent of about 27 locks – and required four men to operate it. A steam engine powered the winding drum.

The **Tar Tunnel** is open to visitors in summertime. The original shaft was opened up in association with the coal mines, and workers were amazed to find natural bitumen flowing from its walls and collecting in pools on the floor. Cauldrons were set up at the tunnel entrance to boil the bitumen, creating pitch for treating ropes and wood. It was even bottled as 'British Oil', a remedy for rheumatism!

Wenlock Edge

Walking on the Bottom of the Sea

Look out for fossils in the scree that litters the path

It's an amazing thought that 400 million years ago the ridge of land we call Wenlock Edge was a coral reef at the bottom of a tropical sea! Gradually the land mass drifted north and an upheaval of the earth's crust tilted the layers, yet still today we can see that the rock of the Edge is limestone composed of the crushed shells of millions of tiny sea creatures. So there you have it, a coral reef in the middle of Shropshire!

It seems very strange to think of being under the sea because in practice the path wanders along the crest of the Edge, with some good viewpoints. Other interesting features are two quarries (one still working), a series of lime kilns that can be explored and a flock of horned black Hebridean sheep that graze the steep quarry sides. It really is a walk for the sharp-eyed, because the woodland of the Edge is especially renowned for its large population of dormice. You haven't much chance of spotting them because they are shy and nocturnal, but you can tell they are there by the particular way they have gnawed the hazel nutshells.

Kiddiwalks in Shropshire

14

Length of walk 2 miles.
Time You *could* walk it in an hour, but allow a lot more time for hunting.
Terrain Well-defined woodland paths with some steps. Not suitable for pushchairs.

Start/Parking Presthope National Trust free car park (GR: SO 583975).
Map OS Explorer 217 The Long Mynd & Wenlock Edge.
Refreshments No facilities on the walk, but there are plenty of tearooms and pubs in Much Wenlock.

1 Take the gravelled path from the back of the car park, where arrows indicate three different walks. Very soon you have a fine view out to the Stretton Hills and

The Walk

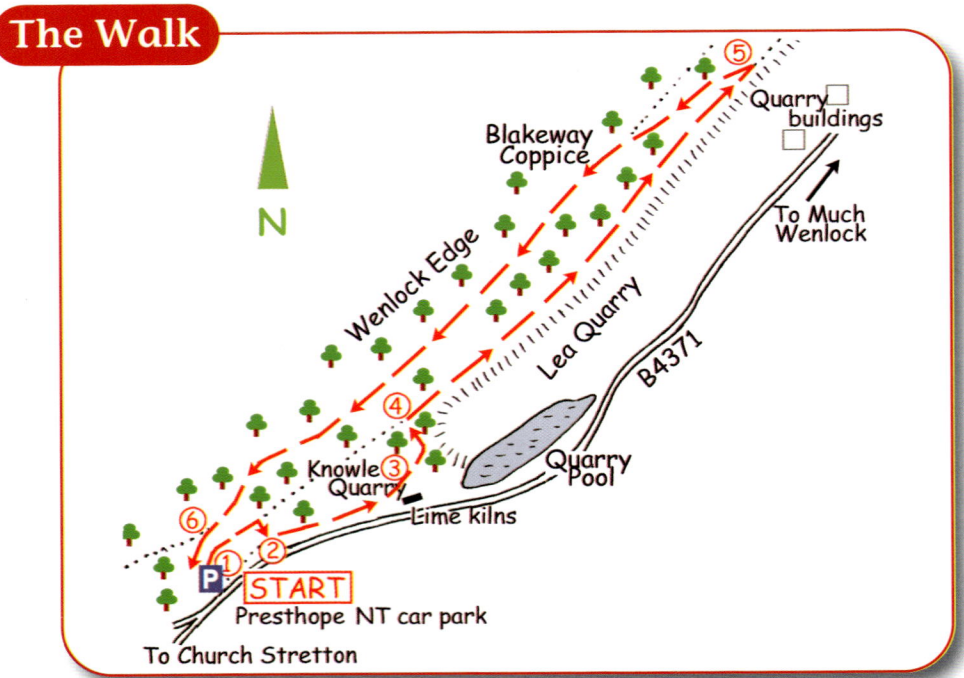

the Long Mynd. Further on, fork right, following a purple arrow.

2 After about 100 yards, turn left down steps (leaving the purple route). The path now parallels the road, then drops down steeply into disused Knowle Quarry. Take time to read the information panel showing you the sort of grey rock that was the original reef. Continue on the obvious path to reach a junction above some lime kilns.

◆ Fun Things to See and Do ◆

 If the children have seen pictures of a coral reef, they will know how pretty it is, with colourful creatures swimming and crawling all around it. Those lumps of dark grey rock don't fit the bill somehow! But looking carefully, you should be able to see glints of shells in the rock – taking a magnifying lens might help. Almost any rock you pick up will have some **shell fragments or coral patterns** in it. But don't set your hearts on too perfect a fossil because plenty of people have been here before. Fossils are real treasures that other people would like to see too, so you should not take home with you more than you can carry in one hand.

Finding **nuts nibbled by dormice** is another hunting game. Squirrels tend to crack their nuts, while dormice, mice and voles gnaw round holes through their shells. Dormice classically leave those holes perfectly smooth on the inside, with diagonal teethmarks on the outside. Can you spot any like that? There aren't that many dormice left in England, so it's a real privilege to get so close to them on Wenlock Edge.

With all that searching, can the children possibly want more for an **Extra Challenge**? At least they can take their eyes off the ground to find these: **a horseshoe on a signpost**, **a wood carving of a trilobite 'fossil'**, **a black sheep**, **a squirrel** and **a log-stack**. If anyone spots all those and has a fossil and a nut to take home, they most certainly are a first class hunter!

3 The path ahead leads to the base of the kilns, where there is more information. When you have investigated, return to the junction and continue on the uphill path. It passes through an area of coppiced hazel trees with plenty of undergrowth, just what the dormice like best. This is the spot to hunt for those gnawed nuts!

4 At the path junction at the top of the hill, turn right on a track running above functional Lea Quarry. On the left of this track are layers of limestone and, among them, grey solid balls of rock ('ballstones') that were the once the reef. In the fallen rocks you should be able to find fossils. Continue on this balcony path until you are level with the quarry buildings.

5 Now turn sharp left, taking a path plunging into the dense trees of Blakeway Coppice. Turn left on the wide track at the bottom of the slope, and continue through the woodland for about ¾ mile.

6 At the path junction, turn left uphill on a sunken track to return to the car park.

◆ Background Notes ◆

Wenlock Edge is about 18 miles long. It belongs to the Silurian period when sea levels were rising, and Shropshire was under shallow seas south of the Equator. The Edge is in fact the most famous Silurian site in the world, and a subdivision of the Silurian (between 424 and 430 million years ago) has been named the 'Wenlockian'. The fossils found here are mainly of coral (pitted or tiny shells), crinoids (tubular creatures) and brachiopods (shell-shaped, like clams). The museum in Much Wenlock Tourist Information Centre has lots of fossil information, so a visit there first could be worthwhile.

Dormice are tiny (much less than an ounce in weight) and spend about three-quarters of their lives sleeping. In Britain they are a protected species, their numbers having declined seriously over the last century due to loss of suitable habitat. Shropshire has a special conservation plan for its remaining colonies of dormice.

15

Stiperstones

Magic on the Mountain

The dramatic Manstone Rock

Stiperstones is a magic place! It really is – but as long as you don't actually sit on the Devil's Chair or visit Manstone Rock on the longest night of the year when the witches come out you shouldn't have a problem! Of course, there's always Wild Edric, who you might hear banging away in the lead mines beneath the hill, but he's harmless …

The long ridge of Stiperstones with its strange outcrops of quartzite has sparked off many local legends that children will revel in. At 536 m (1,758 ft), it is Shropshire's second highest hill, although it is very easily climbed. The summit point is Manstone Rock, so remember to take a photo, and maybe produce one or two small treats for reward. A little encouragement may mean you have a future Chris Bonington on your hands! And don't think the fun is all over when you leave. The next outcrop is the Devil's Chair (don't sit down!), after which the downhill path crosses fields of springy turf, great for running and leaping. The final stretch is on an all-ability trail with some interesting wind-up boxes delivering sounds of local wildlife.

Kiddiwalks in Shropshire

15

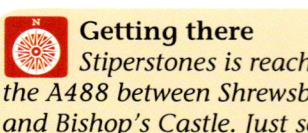

Getting there
Stiperstones is reached off the A488 between Shrewsbury and Bishop's Castle. Just south of Minsterley (at Plox Green), turn off southwards and continue for about 5 miles. With the Bog visitor centre on your right, bear left, and in ½ mile, left again.

Length of walk 3½ miles. Youngest families could simply walk up to Manstone Rock and back – a total distance of about 1½ miles.

Time Allow 2½ hours for the whole walk.

Terrain Manstone Rock is easily accessed, but the ridge path is rough and stony, meaning that the whole route is most suitable for older children. The return is on well-defined tracks. Only the all-ability trail is pushchair-friendly.

Start/Parking The Knolls free car park (GR: SO 369977).

◆ Fun Things to See and Do ◆

Tell the children some of the **legends associated with Stiperstones** – and make sure you **listen for Wild Edric's men** as you go!

Beyond Manstone Rock the path has many protruding stones, so is not ideal for those still in the stumbling stage. But older children will enjoy the feeling of being **'on top of the world'** and having a real bird's-eye view of farms and fields below. Once off the uneven track they can **race downhill** and almost take-off!

The all-ability trail has **curious boxes** that, after vigorous rotation of the handle, tell you something about local bird song. Guaranteed to work off any excess energy!

And of course, there must be an **Extra Challenge**. See how many of the following the children can spot – **a cairn, a sign with a white buzzard logo, a buzzard itself** (look it up before you go), **a notice in Braille, a blue arrow**. Anyone who sees them all deserves a big pat on the back!

The Walk

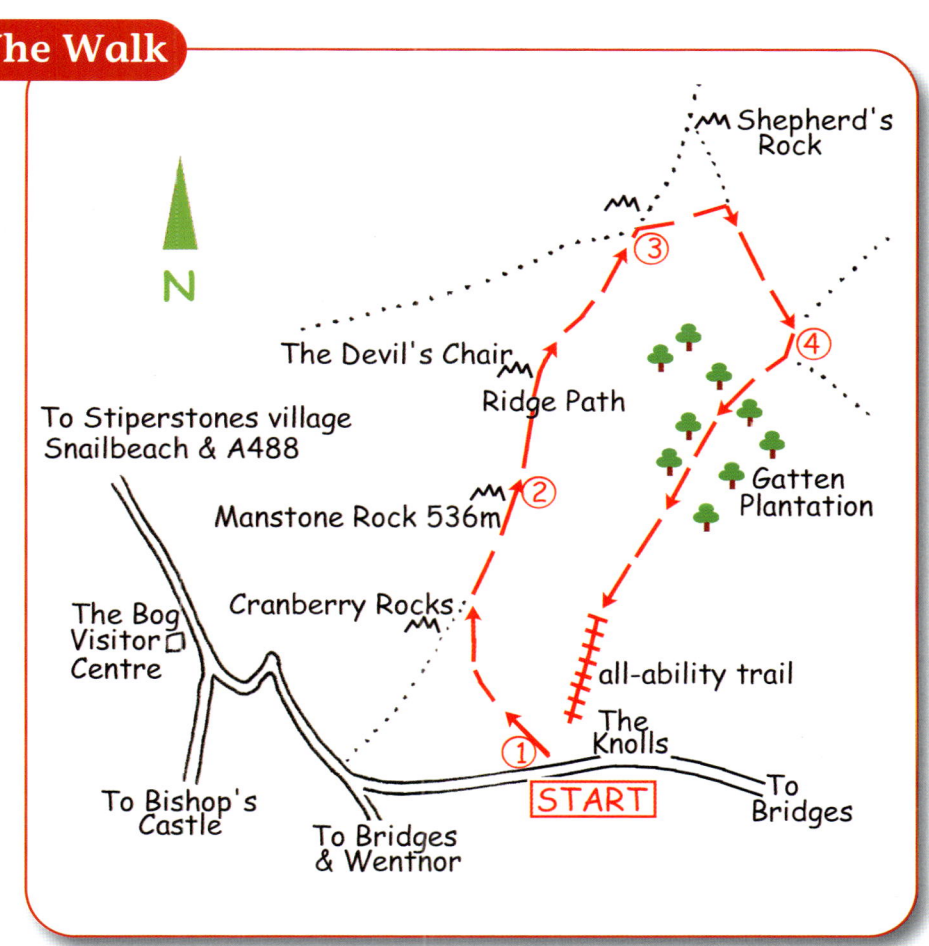

Shepherd's Rock

③

The Devil's Chair

④

Ridge Path

To Stiperstones village
Snailbeach & A488

Gatten
Plantation

Manstone Rock 536m ②

Cranberry Rocks

The Bog
Visitor
Centre

all-ability trail

The
Knolls

①

START

To Bishop's
Castle

To Bridges
& Wentnor

To Bridges

N

Map OS Explorer 216 Welshpool & Montgomery or 217 The Long Mynd & Wenlock Edge.
Refreshments Wonderful cakes (with tea, ice-cream etc.) at the Bog visitor centre, open March to October. Otherwise, the Stiperstones Inn (in Stiperstones village) serves refreshments all hours.

1 Leave the car park via the mountain gate and climb the grassy slope to meet the stony track at a cairn. The outcrop on the left is Cranberry Rocks. Turn

Winding the sound box on the all-ability trail

right and continue uphill past a thick rocky finger to the next outcrop, Manstone Rock. The hill's highest point is actually the trig point on its summit.

2 Take the photocall on the ground – climbing to the trig point is truly at your peril! To continue the walk, keep on the broad rocky ridge path to the next outcrop, the Devil's Chair (which doesn't even seem chair-shaped!). Continue along the rough path, dropping eventually to a junction marked with a cairn (just before a flat-topped rock formation).

3 Turn right here and descend to a path junction beside a gate. Go through the gate, then down the field to another gate. Now bear diagonally right to the field corner.

4 Bear right through a gap in the gorse bushes to a wide track going uphill into Gatten Plantation. Continue through the woodland, then out along the flank of the hill. A section on the all-ability trail returns you to the car park.

◆ Background Notes ◆

The projecting shards of **quartzite** on Stiperstones are in fact the baked sands of a beach of about 500 million years ago! Unique in the area, they naturally engendered a whole crop of **legends**. The Devil apparently holds court from his chair, and is so possessive of it that if anyone else should dare to sit there, he immediately conjures up a thunderstorm. Manstone Rock is said to be the gathering point for witches and ghosts, who frolic there on the longest night of the year. Wild Edric was a Saxon chieftain, who for making peace with the Normans was imprisoned with his men in the lead mines beneath the hill. He is allowed out only in the hour of England's greatest need – and it seems that he was seen in both 1914 and 1939!

Views from the ridge path include the whaleback of the Long Mynd across the valley on the right, with, further ahead, the lonely hump of the Wrekin. On the opposite side is flat-topped Corndon, the site of a prehistoric axe factory. Further back (to its right) Rodney's Pillar in the Breidden Hills is recognised by its abrupt outline, while furthest away are the Berwyns.

Much of Stiperstones is a **National Nature Reserve**. Wildlife includes grouse, buzzards, meadow pipits, ravens, purple-hairstreak butterflies and others – it's worth getting the children to keep their eyes open. In recent years, a 'Back to Purple' initiative has been returning the land to its natural heather and whinberry cover. In August the bright purple slopes of the Stiperstones are a glorious sight.

Lead has been mined in the area since Roman times, the last mine closing in the 1950s. Shropshire Mines Trust have taken over the old mining site at Snailbeach (at the north end of Stiperstones) and invested it with information panels. A blacksmith's forge and a section of a tunnel are open to the public on summer Sundays.

Carding Mill Valley

A Walk on the Wilder Side

Strolling down the valley

Carding Mill Valley is surely the prettiest spot on the Long Mynd, perfect for a family day out. This walk follows a silvery mountain stream up its steep-sided valley to 13 ft high Lightspout Waterfall. It was a spot much loved by the Victorians who would wander up here in full-bustle dresses and tailcoats to admire the scene! A scramble up the rocks alongside the fall (not difficult, or dangerous) soon has you on the wild moorland above where skylarks sing and bilberry and heather blaze with colour in late summer. When you return to the Carding Mill Valley there are pleasant spots to picnic on the grassy banks of the stream while the children paddle and play. And should the weather not be up to alfresco dining, the adjacent National Trust restaurant compensates admirably.

Length of walk 3 miles.

Time Allow 2 hours.

Terrain Rocky paths through the valleys, grassy tracks over the moorland. Ascent and descent steepish in places. The whole route is probably suitable for age 6 years upwards – younger families might like to return directly from the waterfall.

Start/Parking National Trust car parks, both before and beyond the Chalet Pavilion (GR: SO 443945). Parking charge for non-members – members leave their membership cards on the dashboard.

Map OS Explorer 217 The Long Mynd & Wenlock Edge.

Refreshments The National Trust Chalet Pavilion cooks fresh soup and a casserole every day. Alternatives are sandwiches and home-baked cakes, and there are attractively-boxed lunches for children. Open March to November every day 11 am to 4 pm (5 pm in summer), and weekends only in winter.

1 Starting from any of the car parks, walk up Carding Mill Valley beside the stream.

The Walk

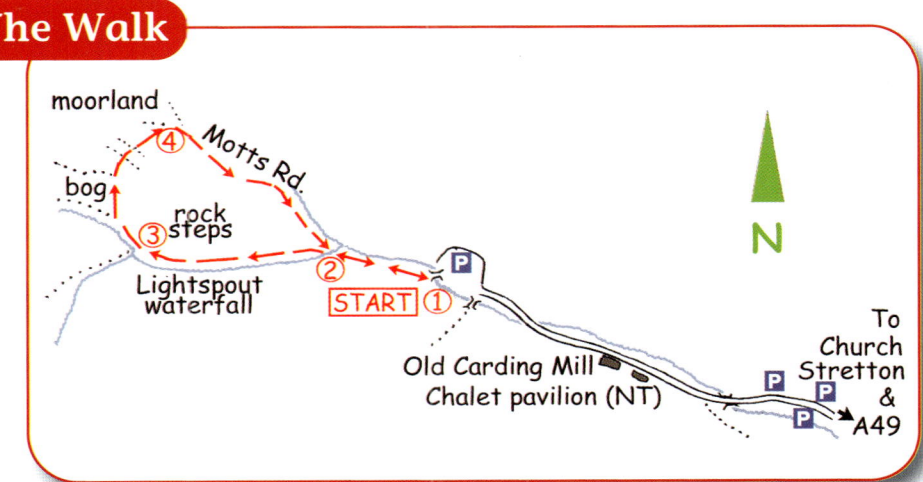

Kiddiwalks in Shropshire

2 At the point where streamlets join, go left up some rough-hewn steps to follow the path beside the larger streamlet. The valley is narrow at first, but widens a little before you reach Lightspout Waterfall. Now climb up the rocky steps to the right of the fall and descend a little to pick up the path beside the stream again.

◆ Fun Things to See and Do ◆

Children will love the adventure of this walk. The path up the valley is narrow and rocky and requires just a little scrambling but never anything dangerous. Can they imagine the immaculately dressed Victorians coming up here? Youngsters will need to be watched on the rocky climb beside the waterfall, but it is a challenge easily met (and enjoyed) by children 5 or 6 years old or more.

If you are here in summertime listen for the **skylarks** on the high plateau. They hover in the air as they sing, but you need sharp eyes to spot them because they are so tiny. There may well be **buzzards** overhead, too.

In August and September the **bilberries** will be ripe. They are quite nice to eat, but lead to blue-stained fingers and blue teeth! Bilberries were once used as a dye, so just make sure no one gets blue-stained clothes as well. Years ago people used to think eating bilberries made them see better in the dark.

For the **Extra Challenge** on this walk, see if anyone can spot: **a sign with a horseshoe**, **some sheep's wool** (not on a sheep!), **heather**, **a holly tree** and **a buzzard**. Congratulations are in order for those who get them all!

And finally, if it's a glorious day, make sure there's time for simply **playing in the water**. These mountain streams are clean and clear – just right for dipping the toes in, racing twigs, or creating dams. Have fun!

3 On reaching a post with a yellow arrow where streams join, keep right. Continue on the main path, finally bearing right to climb above a boggy area. The path now rises gently onto the high moorland. Ignore all grassy cross-tracks until you reach a clear gravelled path.

4 This is Motts Road, an ancient route that is well used today. Turn right and descend beside another stream to reach point 2 and the Carding Mill Valley again.

◆ Background Notes ◆

Carding Mill Valley is named after the huge old mill near the present day Chalet Pavilion. Now converted to luxury apartments, it was originally used for 'carding', the process of combing out the knots in wool ready for spinning.

'Mynd' is the same word as the Welsh *mynydd*, mountain. The **Long Mynd** fits its name well because it is a ridge about 7 miles in length and barely 3 miles wide. The summit is a moorland plateau that rises gently to a highest point of 516 m (1,693 ft). The western flank of the Long Mynd is smooth, with all the wild exciting valleys on the east side. Geologists are particularly fascinated by these valleys, because the old Precambrian rock has been bent upwards in more recent upheavals and in places it lies exposed on the surface in strata that are nearly-vertical. You can see some of these on the walk, and older children might be interested in the explanation. If you turn left instead of right at point 4, Motts Road will take you to the **Portway**, an ancient trackway along the top of the ridge. Alongside the Portway are Bronze Age dykes and many ancient burial chambers.

Since 1965 much of the Long Mynd has been in the care of the National Trust, who strive to protect its **fragile ecology and rare wildlife**. Birds include red grouse and ring ouzel, and plants, bog asphodel and sundew. Other inhabitants are the wild ponies – thought to be descendants of Welsh pit ponies.

Bury Ditches

Now Where Did I Put That Axe-head?

On the ramparts

There are very many hill forts in Shropshire, but Bury Ditches is the biggest and the best! With triple and quadruple ramparts to run up and down, two entrances to find, and a toposcope to point out all the peaks on a 360° horizon, there is plenty to keep everyone amused. And of course the children can also imagine what life might have been like in this lofty place some 2,000 years ago. But this walk has an added dimension. The signboard at the car park tells the story of Llew, an Iron Age boy, who has somehow managed to lose four of his father's prized possessions while playing round the hill fort. Can you help him find them? They are there all right, but you will need sharp eyes to spot them!

Getting there *Bury Ditches lies south of Bishop's Castle via the B4385 – turn off at Brockton and continue through Lower Down to reach the car park on the right. From Craven Arms take the B4368 towards Clun. At Clunton, turn opposite the Crown Inn (signed to Bury Ditches) and continue for about 3 miles (car park on the left).*

Length of walk 1½ miles (two longer routes are also waymarked).

Time Allow an hour.
Terrain Grassy track through the hill fort, otherwise hard-surfaced. Just possible for all-terrain pushchairs.
Start/Parking The free car park for Bury Ditches (GR: SO 334839).
Map OS Explorer 216 Welshpool & Montgomery.
Refreshments There are picnic tables at the car park. The nearest hot food is at the Crown Inn in Clunton. Alternatively, Clun has several pubs and teashops.

1 From the car park, take the

The Walk

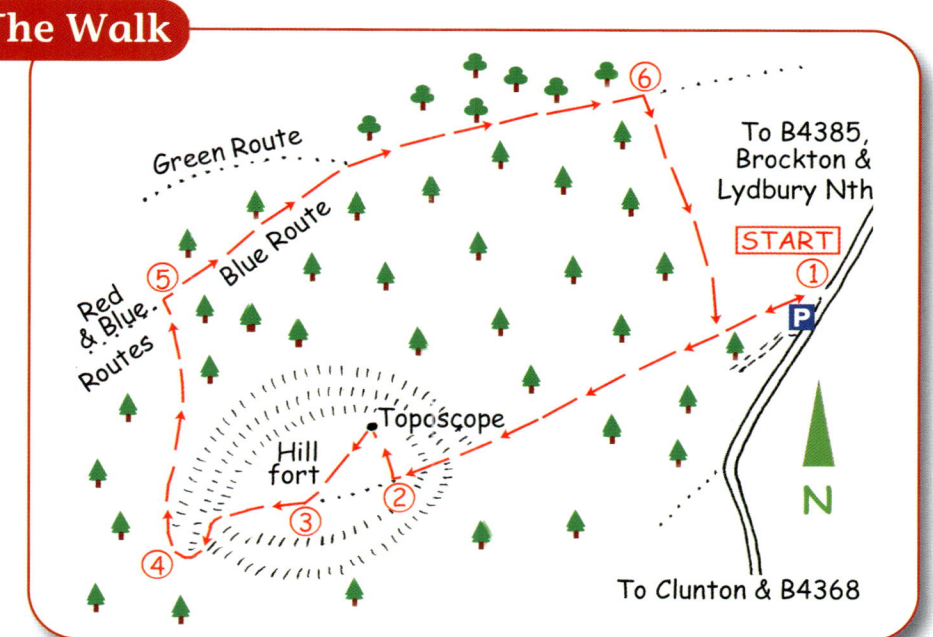

Kiddiwalks in Shropshire

uphill gravelled path. Go through a wooden gate between ramparts to enter the hill fort, and continue on the grassy track.

◆ Fun Things to See and Do ◆

Have a look at the display board in the car park before you set off. It describes the fort – and it also tells you about Llew, the ironsmith's son, who carried some of his father's things out to play and then lost them. **An axe-head, a spear-head, a brooch and a bracelet** (called a torc) are missing. You have to look for them as you climb up the steep path – by the time you reach the toposcope you should have found all four. What exactly are you looking for? Well, these are iron objects (not wood carvings) and they are set into posts, logs and anything else you might see alongside the path.

Inside the hill fort, there is a big **carving of Llew and his dog**. Beneath the flap at the back is a picture of the hill fort when people lived here. It seems a windy sort of place for houses of timber and thatch, but the occupants would have had a very good view of enemies approaching, because there were no trees on the hill then.

Allow a little time to linger in the area of the **toposcope**. All the hills on the horizon are identified. The northern ramparts are close by and the children could have fun running up and down or along the top. You could easily find a sheltered spot for a picnic here.

This walk has offered its own challenge of objects to find, but for the rest of the route here is an **Extra Challenge** – to **count how many signposts** (posts with the coloured footprint symbols) are passed between leaving the toposcope and rejoining the main track at point 5 (don't include the post on the main track here). There are such a lot that it is very easy to lose count – the answer is in Background Notes (*), along with the locations of the lost possessions. Those who found everything **and** got the answer right should go to the top of the class!

Llew, the Iron Age boy

2 Opposite a carving of Llew with his dog, turn right to reach the toposcope. The view is great, and you can maybe climb some of the nearby ramparts. When ready to leave, look back at the path you came on and then take the next path to its right. It leads to a signpost (just visible) on the main track again.

3 At the signpost turn right and walk downhill to pass through the south-west entrance of the fort.

4 Through the gate, turn right

on the forest track, following the waymarks. The track descends through pinewoods to reach a junction.

5 Turn right here, following the blue route (red and green turn left). Soon you are joined by the returning green route and then the track reaches a junction with a gate and open field ahead.

6 Turn right here and continue until you meet the track on which you set out. The car park is about 150 yards to your left.

◆ Background Notes ◆

The Iron Age lasted from approximately 700 BC to AD 43 and Shropshire has about 50 hill forts dating from this time. **Bury Ditches** is now generally regarded as the best example, but curiously, although it was known about, it was completely hidden until recently. The hill on which it stands, Sunnyhill, has long been owned by the Forestry Commission and it was only when severe winter storms in 1978 brought down some trees that parts of the defences were revealed. The Forestry Commission took the hint, and cleared the whole summit of the hill, bringing to light this splendid fort with its three or four layers of high ramparts. The entrances are particularly fascinating. The first entrance (north-east) is 'turned-in' and would probably have had a guard post alongside; the south-west entrance is 'staggered', with the ramparts slotting between each other so that the route in was well overlooked. No excavations have ever been carried out at Bury Ditches. What might lie beneath? By no means everyone in the Iron Age lived in a fort like this. Most people lived in enclosures or simple farmsteads in the valleys. So who were the people who lived here? And why did they need to protect themselves so well?

* There are 9 posts including the last one beside the carving of Llew and his dog (at the junction). The spear-head is behind this carving; the torc is on the long carved log beside the uphill track; the axe-head is on the gatepost at the entrance to the fort; the brooch is on the toposcope.

18

Craven Arms

Up the River and Over the Lea

Onny Meadows

Why is water, and particularly flowing water, always so very fascinating? Children will be in their element on this wander through the water meadows beside the River Onny – they can look out for fish, get right down to water-level on the shingly shores, play among the pollarded willows and watch the huge wheel of a former water mill churning on the opposite bank. It's a good thing this walk is short, because it starts from the Secret Hills Discovery Centre, where there is so much more that the youngsters – and their parents – will want to see and do. The indoors exhibition features a full-sized mammoth skeleton and a trip in a virtual hot air balloon, while outside are more riverside paths and meadows where the whole family can play the 'Iron Age Challenge' game.

Kiddiwalks in Shropshire

18

Getting there *Craven Arms is 7 miles south of Church Stretton on the A49. The entrance to the Secret Hills Discovery Centre is just south of the crossroads in the centre of town.*

Length of walk 2 miles.
Time Allow 1½ hours.
Terrain Field paths – be prepared for some muddy patches after heavy rain. Not suitable for pushchairs (stiles, kissing gates).
Start/Parking Parking area (free) at the Secret Hills Discovery Centre, Craven Arms (GR: SO 435824).
Map OS Explorer 217 The Long Mynd & Wenlock Edge.
Refreshments There is a café serving home-cooked local produce (and snacks) at the Secret Hills Centre.

❶ Facing the Centre, take the path on the left-hand side going into the meadows behind. Now follow the 'Riverside Ramble' signs, pointing you left through a kissing gate into a lane. Keep straight ahead at the lane junction (there are some beautiful old half-timbered cottages here) to cross over the Onny on a white metal bridge.

❷ In the field on the far side, keep to the left, beside the woodland of willows and alders. Aim for a large red-brick house and you will arrive at a stile beside a bridge on Corvedale Road.

❸ Cross the bridge and then the road to arrive at another stile taking you

The Walk

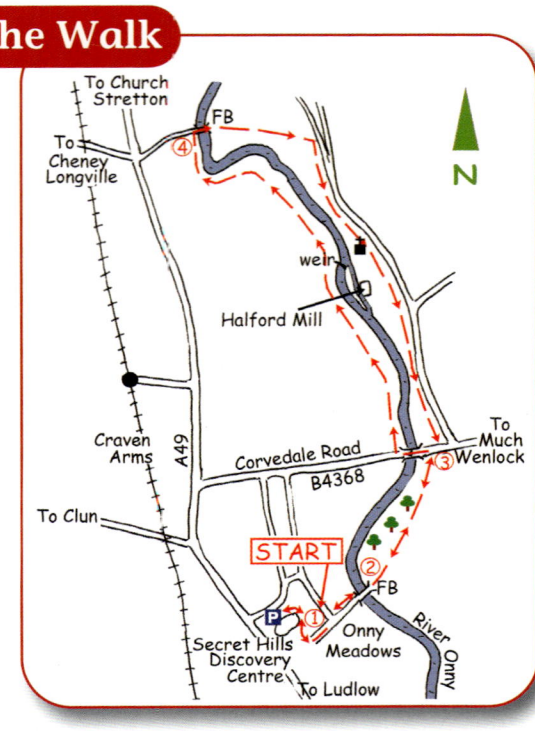

To Church Stretton
FB
To Cheney Longville
④
weir
Halford Mill
N
To Much Wenlock
Craven Arms
A49
Corvedale Road
B4368
③
To Clun
START
②
FB
P
①
Onny Meadows
River Onny
Secret Hills Discovery Centre
To Ludlow

into a riverside meadow once more. This meadow has a strange wiggly depression across it, with one or two old willows alongside. This was obviously the course of the river at some time – was it altered to provide for the mill you can see on the opposite bank? The weir just beyond the mill would have been installed to create a mill pond. Continue beside the meandering river, passing aged broken willows, until you reach a kissing gate at the far end of the field.

◆ Fun Things to See and Do ◆

Where the pools are bright and deep,
Where the grey trout lies asleep,
Up the river and o'er the lea,
That's the way for Billy and me.

That little poem (*A Boy's Song* written in the early 19th century by Scottish poet James Hogg) fits this walk very well. There *are* trout in the River Onny – and roach, and grayling and pike, too. The best place to **spot the fish** is from the bridges where you can look straight down into the clear water.

Other wildlife to look out for on this walk are the **birds that inhabit riversides** like this. You can tell the pied wagtail from the way his long tail bobs furiously up and down, and the dipper is easily recognised by his bright white bib front. Most rare and magical of all is the kingfisher – all you may see is a flash of electric blue as he skims the water.

You can see there's plenty to look out for on this walk, but just to keep everyone really busy, here's the **Extra Challenge**. Try spotting: **a cast iron bell**, **the date 1993**, **a fish**, **a weather vane**, **a horse**. If anyone also sees **a wagtail**, **a dipper** or **a kingfisher**, they are really sharp-eyed – perhaps they deserve an extra reward on arrival back at the Secret Hills Centre!

4 Turn right to cross the white bridge, and then bear right to cross the field on a gravelled path. On its far side, turn right on the lane, continuing ahead on the little metalled road through the peaceful village of Halford. Keep ahead at the junction to meet Corvedale Road again. The stile at point 3 is just 100 or so yards along the pavement to the right, and from there you can return to the Centre the way you came.

◆ Background Notes ◆

The **Secret Hills Discovery Centre** is a curious building – low, grass-roofed and without a straight line anywhere. The explanation is that it was designed to represent an Iron Age hill fort, of which Shropshire boasts more than 50. Inside the Centre, which is open daily throughout the year, there is a café, a shop and an exhibition area. The balloon ride and mammoth skeleton may well be the most memorable features for the youngsters, but there is also a lot about the remarkable geology of Shropshire, and more about its history and folklore. All is presented in a very child-friendly way, with lots of buttons to press and handles to pull. The 30 acres of Onny Meadows outside the Centre likewise appeal to families, with hard surfaced paths (suitable for pushchairs) winding beside the river, a platform looking out over a reed-fringed lake, open fields for play and scattered pieces of adventure equipment. Added to all that, the shop offers a variety of activities, quizzes, trails and challenges that all the family can join in. How about hiring a GPS and going off into the hills to find real treasure? It's possible!

Ludlow

From Castle to Common

Admiring the scene from Ludford Bridge

Ludlow Castle is perfect for children. Now almost 1,000 years old and no more than a huge crumbling ruin, there are still enough secret rooms, slit-like windows, narrow passages and spooky spiral staircases to set the youngsters' imagination blazing. And when all the castle's possibilities have been exhausted, this short walk will complete the day.

The castle looks over the River Teme, and on its far side is fascinating Whitcliffe Common. Paths wind up through woods where leaves lie thick on the ground and wildlife abounds. Beneath some of the trees are trenches said to have been made by the Parliamentarians when they were besieging the castle in 1646 – you can imagine the scene! And at the top of the hill the grassy plateau offers the most fabulous view of town and castle. 'Probably the loveliest town in England' was John Betjeman's verdict on Ludlow. When everyone is ready to go home you can make your way back through its delightful old streets to return to the castle.

Kiddiwalks in Shropshire

19

Getting there *Ludlow is in the far south of the county and the walk starts from the centre of town.*

Length of walk 2 miles.
Time Allow 1½ hours.
Terrain Hard-surfaced paths and pavements. Suitable for all-terrain pushchairs (with help on the steps in point 2).
Start/Parking Pay and display parking off Castle Square (GR: SO 510747). Also free parking at Whitcliffe Common for anyone wanting to start

at point 3.
Map OS Explorer 203 Ludlow.
Refreshments There is a tearoom at the castle and plenty more in the town.

1 Facing the castle gate, take the path on the right, which runs below the castle walls. At the fork, descend right to join the road where two mills once stood beside Dinham Bridge. Cross the bridge and go straight ahead into the lower level of Whitcliffe Common.

2 Here there are three paths, all interesting. The left one,

The Walk

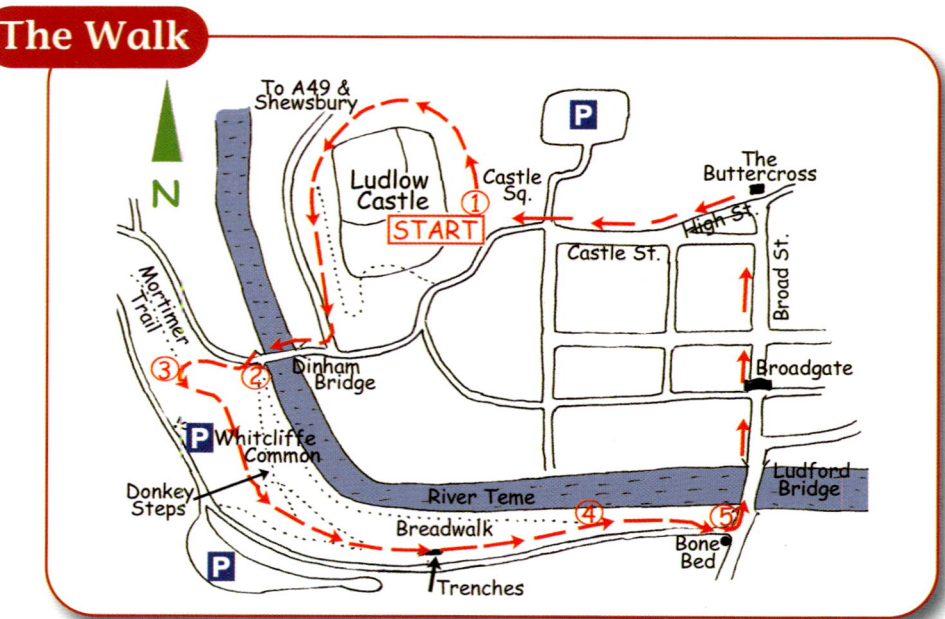

alongside the river, is called the Breadwalk because the workmen who created it in the 1850s were actually paid in bread rather than money. The next path on the left is the 'Donkey Steps', the route used by packhorses carrying iron ore from the Clee Hills. The right-hand path is the route of the long-distance Mortimer Trail. This is the path you want and it climbs steeply up a series of steps (how many are there?). After levelling off, there are a few more steps before reaching a path junction.

3 Turn left here, leaving the Mortimer Trail. The path continues through the woods until eventually a grassy area slopes up on the right. Walk

◆ Fun Things to See and Do ◆

Whitcliffe Common was once a cliff on the edge of a subtropical sea just south of the Equator. Can the children imagine being here then – everyone would have needed their swimwear and sunglasses! But this was around 425 million years ago when there were no people on the earth, only sea creatures and very little land-life. The fossils of those creatures are in the rock beneath your feet. When you get to point 5, take a glance to the right. The rock behind the bench doesn't look much but it has been called the **Ludlow Bone Bed** because it is entirely made up of crushed fish bones.

The grassy top of the common is great for **running and playing games**, with nearby trees for **hide-and-seek**. This could be the spot to have a picnic. And a little further along, you must look out for those **Parliamentarian trenches**. There were fewer trees on the common then and the army would have been looking straight across at Ludlow Castle. Can the children picture it?

Finally, here's the **Extra Challenge**. Keep eyes peeled for **a bat box, a St George's flag, 4 red dragons on a door, a weir** and **a golden weather vane**. Anyone who spots all those must be sharp as a needle!

across the grass and take a rest on one of the benches – the view across the town with Clee Hill in the background is quite magnificent. At the top of this field is a toposcope. When ready, continue on the path skirting the lower edge of the field, then bending around the head of a valley. After passing through a small field, look to the right for those Parliamentarian trenches.

Ludlow Castle seen from Whitcliffe Common

4 The Breadwalk path joins you here. Carry on ahead to meet the road and then walk downhill to the road junction (the Bone Bed is on your right).

5 Turn left, cross the river bridge with care and go straight ahead under the arch of Broadgate to enter the town. Walk up Broad Street and turn left in front of the handsome Buttercross (originally a butter market) to return to Castle Square.

◆ Background Notes ◆

Ludlow Castle was begun in 1086 by Roger de Lacy, a Marcher Lord. Some 200 years later Roger Mortimer enlarged it and later still the castle came into the possession of the Crown. Under Edward IV it achieved great importance as the headquarters of his new Council of the Marches of Wales and royalty made frequent visits to Ludlow. The castle fell into disrepair after William and Mary abolished the Council in 1689. The castle's website www.ludlowcastle.com will give you details of opening times and admission charges.

So remarkable are the rock faces of Whitcliffe that a special **Geology Trail** has been created to demonstrate them. The work of geologist Sir Roderick Murchison in the 19th century resulted in a special division of the Silurian period, known as the Whitcliffian.

Severn Valley Country Park

By River and Rail

Setting off on an adventure!

I t's hard to imagine that the Severn Valley Country Park was once the site of a huge coal mine – or rather, two mines, one on either side of the river! But nature has amazing powers to regenerate and – with a little help from man – open grassland, coppiced woodland, reed-fringed lakes and riverside meadows now fill the scene. Children can enjoy themselves here. The woods are magically filled with streams and waterfalls, and there are little coloured arrows to follow as you make your way on winding paths to the banks of the Severn. Beside the great river the meadows are springy underfoot and there are herons and other waterfowl to spot. The bonus is the Severn Valley Railway that runs right through the park. Steam engines huff and puff along beside you near the end of this walk, a great incentive for young railway enthusiasts!

Kiddiwalks in Shropshire

20

Getting there *The Severn Valley Country Park is near the village of Alveley, about 6 miles south of Bridgnorth. From the A442, brown signs direct you through the village and down a winding lane to the entrance.*

Length of walk 2½ miles.
Time Allow 2 hours.
Terrain Woodland paths and hard-surfaced tracks. Some steps. Possible alternatives for pushchairs.
Start/Parking The visitor centre near the free car park at the country park (GR: SO 753840).
Map OS Explorer 218 Wyre Forest & Kidderminster.
Refreshments There is a teashop at the visitor centre offering sandwiches made to your requirements, home-made cakes, soup, ice-creams and other snacks. Open throughout the year Wednesday to Sunday and bank holidays – and every day in school holidays, 12 noon to 5 pm (4 pm in winter).

1 From the front of the visitor centre follow the green arrows of the Woodland Trail across the grass to the left. Cross the metalled path and continue along the woodland edge. Soon the green arrows direct you right over a wooden bridge across a little stream. After going through a kissing gate bear right into the wood, still following the green arrows. The path bends right, then reaches a track junction.

2 The green route turns left here on a short diversion through the coppice. Follow it if you will – but if you keep straight ahead here, you

The Walk

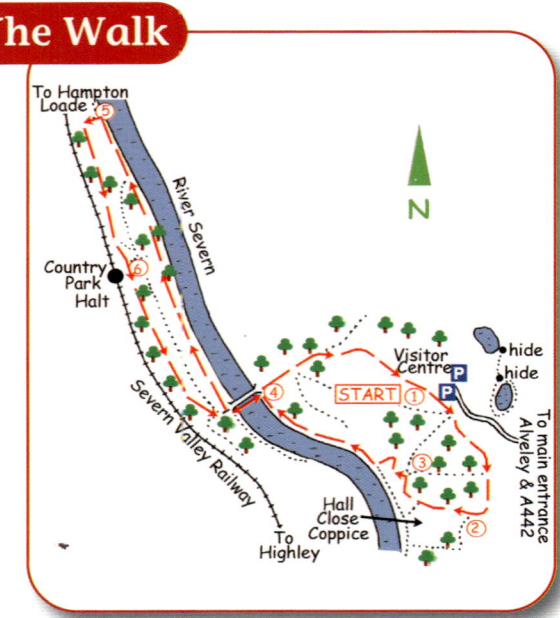

rejoin the green path in a few minutes. Briefly you find you are following both yellow and green.

3 At the next junction turn left with yellow (leaving the green route). The trail passes the site of the old ferryman's house – before

◆ Fun Things to See and Do ◆

The **woodland** is really delightful and every twist and turn of the path reveals a new stream or waterfall. In spring there will be bluebells, primroses or wood anemones to spot, and there are so many birds at home here.

In the fields beside the river are **anthills** made by red meadow ants. The sandy soil here is red too. Can the children think what makes the colour? (The sand grains are cemented together by red iron oxide.)

This waterside area is the place to look out for the big grey **herons** and much tinier **wagtails** and **kingfishers**. There are also **otters** here – you will be very fortunate if you spot one of those. And while in this area, look out for **bunches of mistletoe** in some of the riverside trees. Do the children know how the mistletoe gets its food?

At the end of this walk you will meet the **Severn Valley Railway line**. The trains run at weekends all year round, and on weekdays also in summertime. In peak season there are 7 or 8 trains a day in each direction. Trains stop by request at Country Park Halt – you could consider a trip of a few minutes downline to Highley, where there is lots to see in the newly-opened Engine House

Finally here is the **Extra Challenge** – look out for **a bird nesting box**, **a flood level gauge** (like a ruler), **an image of a blue boat** (a Severn trow), **a red flag** and **a picture of a badger**. Those who spotted them all probably deserve an extra ice-cream back at the visitor centre!

the bridge was built, the crossing here was made by boat. Soon the path corners sharply left, then descends to the banks of the Severn and runs beside the river to the bridge.

4 Go up the steps and cross the bridge. At the far side, take the lowest of the three paths on the right, the one going into the riverside meadow. You are now following blue arrows (the Riverside Trail) and will stick with them all the way home. The path leads across a meadow, through woodland, then across another meadow.

5 Here you leave the riverside and turn left up the steps. Soon the Severn Valley Railway is ahead and the track bears left to

Rustling up the leaves

run parallel to it. After passing a clearing you arrive at Country Park Halt, where trains will stop on request.

6 Continue ahead on the main path to return to the river bridge again. Cross the bridge and, after about 200 yards, bear left. After a further 200 yards, take the right fork and continue climbing uphill to the visitor centre.

◆ Background Notes ◆

Coal mining has been carried on at Highley since the Middle Ages. The latest mine was opened in 1870, and activities were transferred to the Alveley site in 1936. Coal from Highley was transferred by tramway to be loaded onto trains at Highley station, a mile downriver. The path you follow from Country Park Halt was part of the tramway. From the Alveley site, a ropeway slung across the river transported the coal to the opposite bank. The mines finally closed in 1969. In 1986 Bridgnorth District Council and Shropshire County Council joined together to begin the reclamation of the site, which has now earned the prestigious national Green Flag Award.